The Rise of Bishops

The Rise of Bishops

From Parish Leaders to Regional Governors

DAVID W. T. BRATTSTON

Foreword by Manfred W. Kohl

WIPF & STOCK · Eugene, Oregon

THE RISE OF BISHOPS
From Parish Leaders to Regional Governors

Wipf & Stock
An Imprint of Wipf and Stock Publishers
199 W. 8th Ave., Suite 3
Eugene, OR 97401

www.wipfandstock.com

PAPERBACK ISBN: 978-1-6667-0973-5
HARDCOVER ISBN: 978-1-6667-0974-2
EBOOK ISBN: 978-1-6667-0975-9

NOVEMBER 3, 2021

Citations of Cyprian in Latin are from Wilhelm August Hartel S. *Thasci Caecili Cypriani* : Opera omnia / *recensvit et commentario critico* (Vindobonae : apvd C. Geroldi filivm, 1868–71). Series: Corpus scriptorum ecclesiasticorum Latinorum (abbreviated "CSEL"), vol. 3.

Dedicated to
Dr. Barbara Marie Kohl
of Blandford, Nova Scotia

The problem of Church Order revolves around the office of the bishop.
—W. H. C. FREND, *THE EARLY CHURCH*

Contents

Permissions

Except where otherwise indicated, all Bible quotations are from the Authorized (King James) version.

The authors assert moral rights under the laws of Canada and reciprocating jurisdictions.

Except where otherwise indicated, all patristic quotations are as translated in *The Ante-Nicene Fathers: Translations of the Writings of the Fathers Down to A.D.* 325, edited by Alexander Roberts and James Donaldson. American Reprint of the Edinburgh edition by A. Cleveland Coxe (Buffalo, NY: Christian Literature, 1885–96; continuously reprinted with Edinburgh: T. & T. Clark; Grand Rapids: Eerdmans; Peabody, MA: Hendrickson). Herein cited as "ANF."

Except where otherwise indicated, references to and quotations from church councils, and from the historians Socrates Scholasticus, Sozomen, and Theodoret, are from *Nicene and Post-Nicene Fathers Second Series* New York: Christian Literature Co. 1900; reprinted Grand Rapids, MI: Eerdmans, 1983. Herein cited as "NPNF 2d."

References to and quotations from Eusebius's *Ecclesiastical History* are from *Church History of Eusebius*. Translated by Arthur Cushman McGiffert. Nicene and Post-Nicene Fathers Second Series. (New York: Christian Literature; Oxford: Parker, 1890; continuously reprinted with Grand Rapids, MI: Eerdmans; Edinburgh: T. & T. Clark; Peabody, MA: Hendrickson).

Permissions

Some content is reproduced by permission of Resource Publications, an imprint of Wipf and Stock, from the author's *Apostolic Succession: An Experiment that Failed* (2020).

Foreword

I GREW UP IN SOUTHERN GERMANY during the aftermath of the terrible Second World War. Everybody had to deal with guilt, forgiveness, grace, and hope. On Sundays I attended the local church, the Landeskirche (the United Protestant Church—Lutheran and Reformed). The hieratical structure with bishops and National/ State church offices that dealt with all personal issues, finances, church policies, and forms of sacraments and worship was accepted as biblical and ordained by God. Everyone paid a church tax that was collected by the government.

When I began to study church history and biblical theology I came across the Congregational Church Movement (The Pilgrims, the Mayflower, the Puritans, and the Congregationalists). During my theological studies I became fascinated with the simple concept of Congregationalism as they believe to be the same as the early Christians in Jerusalem. After immigrating to America I joined a Congregational Church and later was ordained as Congregational Pastor. I served for years in the First Congregational Church in Middleboro, Massachusetts. This church is only miles away from Plymouth, founded by the second-generation pilgrims that landed in 1620 in America, coming from England via Holland. In the church that I served the basic congregational principal is still practiced: every member in the church has an equal say/vote how the church should function from electing their own pastor to dealing with the form of worship, sacraments, education, property, and finances. In true Congregationalism there is no authority above the local church body.

Dr. David W. T. Brattston, a lawyer, not a theologian, took time to explain in detail how the church structure developed from the first "Mother Church" in Jerusalem to the hieratical concept with policies, oversight, financial structures, and power. The church activities were slowly centralized but moving towards a clear episcopacy structure which developed into the specific papacy concept of Rome. In his latest book, *The Rise of Bishops: From Parish Leaders to Regional Governors*, Brattston begins with the era of the original apostles, referring to the reports given to us in Acts and the writings of Paul, Peter, and John. He gives eight examples how the early church dealt with governance issues, always referring to the leadership of the apostles. One example is how the church in Antioch went to the "Mother Church" in Jerusalem to seek the help from the Apostles Council.

In Brattston's former works: *Papal Supremacy* (2018) and *Apostolic Succession: An Experiment That Failed* (2020) he specifically focused on the important question, "Who replaces the Apostles?" Peter, John, and the other disciples and later Paul were appointed directly by God, filled with divine inspiration and authority.

In the four Gospels there are no specific instructions from Jesus how the disciples should be replaced and how a group of believers/followers should be governed. In the epistles we get some insight how leaders should be appointed. Brattston pointing out that apostles appointed the next generation of elders/leaders (Acts 14:23) and that they in turn should appoint elders/leaders (Titus 1:5). However it was always within the local congregation. It was not until the second and third century that a concept of a bishop who was above the elders was introduced and that one bishop could now be responsible for several congregations.

Brattston went carefully through the writings of all early church fathers of the second and third century to point out how the concept and practice of priests, bishops, leading bishops, and the laity were introduced, however, always with the support of the congregation, the local body of believers. Brattston stated that

before AD 300 the local congregations appear to have been autonomous, administered by bishops and deacons, and sometimes
elders, all as congregational officeholders, with no superstructure
above the congregation. Brattston pointed out that from the fourth
century on the congregations were governed by a hierarchy, from
the top down, including diocesan bishops and metropolitans. His
book deals directly and in depth with the transition from bishops
being interchangeable with local elders to a single bishop for each
congregation, and the later transition to diocesan episcopacy, by
examining painstakingly the writing of the authors of that time in
which the change took place.

For nearly three hundred years the church not only struggled
to survive, it also had to deal with the selection of Holy Script and
its interpretation. The fight of how and who should the church be
governed became one of the major issues. Different alliances were
formed, and power-based groups claimed authority, especially in
the newly established Metropolitans. Bishops of bishops were appointed and they developed a mighty force in the quest of who
has the final authority. Countless councils and meetings took place
to deal with hundreds of issues of church government. Brattston
went into every detail to explain the change and its impact from
the local church authority to regional church authorities to finally
one central authority for the entire church.

Brattston also pointed out that from the beginning Constantine intervened in church affairs with the single purpose of
keeping peace and unity. Eusebius, in *Life of Constantine*, mentioned that when Constantine addressed the Council of Nicaea, he
said, "In my judgment, intestine strife within the Church of God,
is far more evil and dangerous than any kind of war or conflict,
and these our differences appear to me more grievous than any
outward trouble."

It is a joy to read Brattston's book although it is sometimes
heavy reading. One hopes that his next research project in the
early church will deal with issues like the development of Christian art; the concept of possession, marriage, and sexual deviation;

and family with emphasis on children, as well as faith and political engagement.

For me, the emphasis on the congregation, laity, and the local clergy is very important. In the twenty-first century the church is so divided. The Roman Catholics with all their splinter groups, the various Orthodox church groups, and the over forty-six thousand Protestant denominations and church groups, each claiming to have the right church structure and follow the Jesus statement of John 17:21, "That all of them may be one . . ." I am glad to be a Congregationalist.

Manfred W. Kohl, ThD
Ambassador, Overseas Council
President/CEO, Re-Forma
Lausanne Catalyst for Integrity and Anti-Corruption

Introduction

THERE ARE MANY SCHOLARLY, and unscholarly, opinions as to the number, titles, arrangement, and jurisdictions of church officers, some of which are an article of faith as to how God wills the church to be organized today. The apostle Paul mentioned apostles, prophets, evangelists, pastors, teachers, miracles, then gifts of healings, helps, governments, and diversities of tongues (1 Cor 12:28; Eph 4:11). Origen[1] commented on the Ephesians list for the purpose of teaching that such office-bearers needed the gift or grace to perform the duties of it, but is ambiguous and asserts no knowledge that these callings had persisted to the third century.[2] With significant and vocal exceptions, patristic scholars and denominations with an episcopal form of government today generally believe that, at least from the second century, there was the now-familiar threefold ministry of bishops, deacons, and elders.[3] Elders are also called presbyters from the Greek term πρεσβύτερος. Most denominations today continue these offices, sometimes under different titles. The present book mainly examines how they were related vertically, whether they were all equals to each other, or in a hierarchy with the pastors or other leaders from many congregations being subordinate to a diocesan bishop, who was in turn answerable to higher officials or councils above them. This book in effect

1. Thumbnail sketches of ancient authors cited in this book appear in a separate appendix.

2. Origen, *Commentary on Ephesians*, 4:11–12.

3. Frend, *Rise of Christianity*, 139; Moore, "Reflections upon Reflections," 162.

studies whether each congregation was independent of all outside Christians, or were subject to churchmen in distant cities. It traces the changes over time from the first to fourth centuries, detailing the developments witnessed by Christian writers of the relevant time periods, until it reached the diocesan episcopal arrangement current in the fourth century and today in some denominations.

Denominations such as Eastern Orthodox, Oriental Orthodox, Episcopalian, and, in an extended form, the Roman Catholic, continue the hierarchical church structure that was in effect at the end of its development in the fourth century, with one man above another in the arrangement pastor/priest, bishop, archbishop, metropolitan bishop, and primate. Some even believe it existed in the first or second century, and thus is God's model of how it is always to be. There are different theologies, practices, and approaches to the authority and functioning of bishops among these several groups, too many differences and subtilties to be dealt with in a book in the nature as the present one. For a treatment of the authority and functions of bishops in the various denominations with a diocesan episcopacy, written by such bishops, the reader is referred instead to Peter Moore's *Bishops, But What Kind?*

Not all Protestants agree with a supra-congregational officer exercising power over more than one church, but hold to an arrangement of each congregation being independent of others, especially of a bishop (e.g., Baptists), or are organized in a hierarchy of "courts" such as congregational elders as a group under regional associations of elders (presbytery) which in turn participate with elders of a court of wider geographical extent (Presbyterian, Reformed). Congregationalists and presbyterians regard the ancient bishop as always an officer of only one local church, and eschew any hierarchy of persons rather than courts, and in turn argue that this is God's plan for the church age. In such denominations, "each congregation constitutes a distinct diocese."[4] The present book shows how all such views are rooted in history, and how they became such.

---

4. Ware, "Patterns of Episcopacy," 18.

Early congregations were founded in cities and towns; only later did they spread to the surrounding countryside. The centralized nature of parish churches in the middle of the second century is alluded to in Justin Martyr's 1 *Apology* 67: "On the day called Sunday, all who live in cities or in the country gather together to one place."[5] The present book narrates what happened to church organization after congregations grew too large to be accommodated in a single place. It begins with a landscape of autonomous local churches, and traces their eventual loss of independence and their reduction to dependence on a regional authority in the person of a diocesan bishop. This book accounts for how and why the Christian church became hierarchical, and how this development was due to forces Americans today would consider dangerous to both church and civic life.

The following pages will both comfort, discomfort, and surprise Protestant denominations that believe that God in the Bible laid out a definite plan of ecclesiastical polity that we are obliged to accept today and forever. It will have a similar effect on Anglicans and Orthodox of their various shades, and especially Roman Catholics.

---

5. Martyr, 1 *Apol.* 67.

CHAPTER 1

The New Testament Period

CHRISTIAN CONGREGATIONS MENTIONED IN THE New Testament were all directed by and in contact with apostles. Nothing is said about church government without apostles. In addition to the extensive directions in Paul's epistles, the New Testament contains eight examples of some person or organization exercising a degree of control over a congregation, each of whom was an apostle.

First, according to Acts 13:1–3, Paul and companions were commissioned as missionaries by a group of prophets and teachers within the church at Antioch. Acts 14:23 records that Paul and Barnabas in turn ordained elders in every church of a missionary field, but does not comment on the purpose or the powers granted to these new church officers or why they were appointed. Elders/presbyters appear suddenly in the New Testament, without indications in the text of when their office was instituted, why they were appointed, qualifications required, or their duties and responsibilities, until the Pastoral Epistles, late in the development of the first-century church. From Acts 15 it appears they performed some deliberative or legislative role in conjunction with apostles, but the New Testament records them acting in other functions as well, always secondarily to apostles.

Secondly, Colossians is the only epistle of Paul that hints that a church in one town possessed jurisdiction over the congregation in another. It commands the Christians of Colossae: "when this epistle is read among you, cause that it be read also in the church of the Laodiceans; and that ye likewise read the epistle from Laodicea" (4:16). The variety of English meanings of the operative word here (ποιήσατε) neither confirm nor exclude the sense that Colossae held authority over Laodicea. Colossians 4:16 was not cited by any ante-Nicene Christian writing,[1] unless we include the late and spurious *Epistle to the Laodiceans*, of which M. R. James comments, "It is not easy to imagine a more feebly constructed cento of Pauline phrases."[2]

Thirdly, Acts 15:2 speaks of the Antiochenes as going to Jerusalem for the resolution of a dispute, instead of inviting representatives from Jerusalem to Antioch, or meeting in a third, neutral place. They appear to have treated Jerusalem as a mother church, or at least as having some higher status than themselves. In the same way, Colossae could have been the mother church exercising oversight over Laodicea, in the same manner as Rome later exercised over Western Christendom, and diocesan cathedrals over distant congregations. Yet the postbiblical evidence to the middle of the fourth century indicates that whatever oversight there was over congregations and clergy was by councils, where they existed, rather than one congregation subordinate to another.

Fourthly, it appears in Acts 15 that the Council of Jerusalem was held between only two congregations, presbyteries, or dioceses, one at Jerusalem and one at Antioch. Yet the decisions of the Council were distributed as binding on congregations in Syria and Anatolia (15:23–29). The Antiochene church may have represented them, or have been a mother church exercising binding jurisdiction over them, and the Jerusalem church over those in Judaea. Verse 16:4 speaks of the decision as that of "The apostles and elders and brethren" (15:23) or "of the apostles and elders which were at Jerusalem" (16:4). Nor did they consider it to be enough to

1. Biblindex.

2. James, *Apocryphal New Testament*, 479.

entrust the Antiochene delegation with a copy of the decision, but sent leading members of the Jerusalem community to accompany them (15:22, 27). It was not apostles alone who made the decision, but the elders as well, with perhaps further ratification by the Jerusalem laity (brethren). It is unclear whether the elders in Acts 15 held powers approximate to those of later bishops, for we would expect nascent bishops as well as presbyters to be present at such an important conference, if the office of bishop had been instituted this early. Noteworthy here is the observation of Robert M. Grant: "In the New Testament itself the bishop is mentioned in the singular only three times (I Tim. 3:2; Titus 1:7; I Pet. 2:25, of Christ, cf. Ign. *Rom.* 9:1) and in the plural only twice (Acts 20:28; Phil. 1:1)."[3]

The Council of Acts 15 and the composition of 1 Clement took place in the time of the apostles, who had been directly commissioned by Christ and still received visions from him. They could write what later became Scripture, and issue instructions with divine authorization. Their authority was unique, and the postbiblical literature does not contemplate that apostles' supercongregational authority or the office of apostles would continue. The apostles in the Didache exercised no legislative functions but were completely under the control of the host congregation, unlike those in the New Testament. It is anachronistic to project the institutions of the later church into the apostolic age, such as the writer of 1 Clement being in the position of the later bishops of Rome. In fact, 1 Clement may have been written by an apostle rather than, as is generally assumed, by some second-generation officer of the congregation at the city of Rome. It does not indicate what sanctions Rome could impose if the Corinthians failed to heed it. It contains no threat to excommunicate. It could not inflict any penalty, for any punishment or intervention would have come from one of the apostles, some of whom were alive when 1 Clement was written.

First Clement may have been written by the apostle John the Revelator. According to the church father Tertullian, John resided at Rome long enough to be detected as a Christian, escape death during a persecution, and then banished to Patmos. Speaking of City of Rome, Tertullian noted: "where Peter endures a passion like his Lord's! where Paul wins his crown in a death like John's [the Baptist's]! where the Apostle John was first plunged, unhurt, into boiling oil, and thence remitted to his island-exile!"[4] Tertullian wrote this somewhere between AD 198 and 207. This explains why someone in Rome became involved in the deposition of clergy at Corinth, which was much farther from Rome than John's some-time habitation and ministry in Ephesus and the eastern shore of the Aegean. If John was permanently resident at Ephesus, it is odd that he is not mentioned in the Epistle to that church or those to Timothy.

The fifth is 3 John:

> 9 I wrote unto the church: but Diotrephes, who loveth to have the preeminence among them, receiveth us not. 10 Wherefore, if I come, I will remember his deeds which he doeth, prating against us with malicious words: and not content therewith, neither doth he himself receive the brethren, and forbiddeth them that would, and casteth them out of the church.

It appears from this passage that the author's authority was not universally recognized at this time, similar to the situation described in 1 Clement. Third John appears to indicate a nonresident overseer or diocesan bishop in the modern sense with only very limited powers, having authority to intervene in congregational affairs, yet all the author can do is to raise the issue with the congregation; it appears that he possessed no power of his own to excommunicate or depose Diotrephes.

The sixth reference is in the Epistle to Titus, which would indicate a diocesan, episcopal polity, like Roman Catholic, Orthodox, and Anglican structures today. According to the King James Version, Paul purportedly commanded: "For this cause left I thee in Crete, that thou shouldest set in order the things that are wanting, and ordain elders in every city, as I had appointed thee" (Titus

---

4. Tertullian, *Paescr.* 36.

1:5). The Greek root here for "ordain" has a wide range of translations in English New Testaments, the most likely of which is that Titus was commanded to appoint presbyters, not necessarily bishops, and not necessarily without prior approval by the laypeople to be affected. Remember the writer of the letter identifies himself as an apostle.

Seventh, 1 Peter 5:1–2 exhorts elders to be overseers or bishops of their flocks. The word always appears in the plural in the New Testament, with the exceptions of 1 Timothy 3:2 and Titus 1:7, which are clearly generic and outline the qualifications of an individual candidate for the office, not the complete congregational ministry itself.

Eighth, the Revelation to John 2.2: "I know thy works, and thy labour, and thy patience, and how thou canst not bear them which are evil: and thou hast tried them which say they are apostles, and are not, and hast found them liars:" This indicates a degree of chaos or uncertainty in early Church government, confusion as to who was an apostle, and so many apostles that there was room for imposters to insinuate themselves. This should make as wary of claims by anyone after the first century to possess apostolic authority.

First Clement 44.3 states that new elders/bishops after the deaths of apostolic appointees were appointed "with the consent of the whole Church," which indicates that it was God's plan that the laity and presbyters/elders participate in elections to the episcopate. The Epistle states that apostles had ordained their immediate successors, and the officeholders about whom the letter spoke were the successors' successors, or still later in the succession. This is the apostolic succession, which was dependent for its continuance on the consent of the laity, but they could not afterwards depose someone they had elected.

CHAPTER 2

Church Polity in the Second and Third Centuries

Unlike the authors of the New Testament (and perhaps of some "apocryphal" New Testament books), the fathers of the first three centuries lived in a situation more like later eras, including our own. In the four Gospels and other accounts of Jesus and his apostles, disciples were led and taught directly by God manifested in the flesh or by men he had personally selected and had filled with divine inspiration. Just as we do not enjoy these contacts today, neither did any Christians after the death of the last apostle.[1] Indeed, almost all Christian life has taken place in such "uninspired" circumstances. Early postbiblical Christian literature provides a more comparable model for today, a model in which modern spiritual conditions are paralleled but with the added benefit of fresher memories of the sources of the Faith.

OFFICES IN THE CHURCH

The New Testament says nothing about church government after apostles passed from the scene. The commands in it came from

1. Ware, "Patterns of Episcopacy," 1–2.

Jesus or an apostle, not a bishop or presbytery in the modern-day sense. Because of the overarching role of apostles at the time, the New Testament was not a model or precedent for church order in the later periods. The question had become "who replaces the apostles?"

Although nobody between the apostolic era and the fourth century wrote a formal constitution or canons governing the relations of congregations to each other or to a shared overseer/ diocesan bishop, the only conclusion someone can draw from the isolation of congregations from one another, the confusion, the lack of references about the contacts between them, the absence of missionary societies or other joint ventures, and the utter lack of coordination or supervision over them (except, perhaps, 1 Clement) indicate a purely congregational structure, with the local assemblies being totally independent, with no superstructure above the parish.

Modern-day patristic scholars and denominations with an episcopal form of government generally believe that, at least from the second century, there was a divinely-sanctioned ministry of deacons and elders led by bishops. Although it is generally agreed that the day-to-day functioning of individual congregations in the earliest times was by a college or committee of elders, at least in part, it is unclear whether "elder" is always synonymous with bishop or pastor, with a bishop being just another elder among many in New Testament times and, in many places, until the middle of the second century. Paul addressed the "bishops and deacons" in Philippians 1:1, while in letters to other churches he said "elders [presbyters] and deacons." In Acts 20:28, in a speech to the elders of Ephesus, he alluded to the Holy Spirit having made them bishops. First Timothy 3:1–13; 5:17–19; and Titus 1:6–9 give the qualifications for only two offices, bishops and deacons, but later use the term "presbyter" for bishop. The word "presbyter" occurs five times in 1 Clement,[2] each is described as being in exactly the same situation as men it elsewhere calls "bishops," and treats the words as interchangeable. "Bishop" appears only in 42.4–5, three

2. 1 Clem. 1.3, 44.5, 47.6, 54.2, 57.1.

times in the phrase "bishops and deacons," and where other ancient authors would say "elders and deacons."[3]

In the second and third centuries, a bishop was a congregational official. Although a bishop was not distinct from the other elders in the New Testament period nor in Western Europe prior to the middle of the second century, after this period there was only one bishop in a congregation, assisted by presbyters and deacons in an arrangement known as monepiscopacy, adjective monepiscopal. In contrast to a polity of several bishops in one congregation, as equal elders or presbyters, or to one bishop over several congregations, "monepiscopal" indicates the system, introduced in the very late first or early second century, of each congregation having its own bishop and only one bishop. Elders/presbyters, of which there were always more than one in any congregation, began to descend to a secondary status. This polity was first referred to by Ignatius of Antioch around AD 107, in his letters to Polycarp and congregations in the western mainland Turkey. Scholars and writers that comment on the early church believe this development began in Syria and slowly spread westward, reaching the city of Rome in the middle of the second century.

According to Ignatius,

> Let no man do anything connected with the Church without the bishop. Let that be deemed a proper Eucharist, which is [administered] either by the bishop, or by one to whom he has entrusted it. Wherever the bishop shall appear, there let the multitude [of the people] also be; even as, wherever Jesus Christ is, there is the Catholic Church. It is not lawful without the bishop either to baptise or to celebrate a love-feast; but whatsoever he shall approve of, that is also pleasing to God, so that everything that is done may be secure and valid.[4]

Ignatius drew a clear distinction between presbyters and bishops, with only one bishop in a congregation and the elders subordinate to him. First Clement and Ignatius asserted that

3. 1 Clem. 44.1, 4.
4. Ign. *Smyrn.* 8.1.

Christians are duty-bound to obey the incumbents in the existing church order simply because it is the existing order. Neither
nor Ignatius nor 1 Clement stated that the authority of the clergy
is based on divine call, more or exclusive possession of the Holy
Spirit, reception of fresh revelations from heaven, or possession of
an otherwise-unknown body of secret Christian knowledge.

About this time frame, a little earlier or a little later, Didache
15.1 exhorts local Christian congregations themselves, not diocesan bishops or a pope, to select clergy: "Appoint, therefore, for
yourselves, bishops and deacons worthy of the Lord, men meek,
and not lovers of money, and truthful and proved; for they also
render to you the service of prophets and teachers."[5]

According to Professor Peter Stockmeier of the University of
Munich, worship in the church described in the Didache required

> suitable superintendents, men who have . . . attained
> this position by election. According to this instruction
> it is not appointment by existing office-bearers but the
> people's choice—made, admittedly, in accordance with
> specific criteria—which calls a man into the service of
> bishop and deacon.[6]

At early or mid-second-century Rome, Hermas also uses the
term "bishop," but in the plural and once alongside the office of
deacon,[7] and spoke of apostles, bishops, deacons and teachers as
distinct ministries.[8] Clement of Alexandria in Egypt, much farther
east, wrote in the AD 190s of "the grades here in the Church, of
bishops, presbyters, deacons, are imitations of the angelic glory."[9]
Likewise, Origen, his successor as dean of a theological school,
knows only bishops, presbyters, and deacons as church officials,[10]

---

5. Did. 15:2.

6. Stockmeier, "Election of Bishops," 5.

7. Herm. Vis. 3.5.1; Herm. Sim. 9.27.2.

8. Herm. Vis. 3.5.1.

9. Clement of Alexandria, *Strom.* 6.13.

10. Origen, *Hom. Ps. 37*, 1.1, ll. 144–46.

as late as the time of Cyprian.[11] As for the nature of the bishop as an officer of only one congregation in contrast to a diocese of several,

> It should be remembered, of course, that the single bishop in the early church was much more like the minister of one of our city parishes than like the diocesan bishop of to-day. Otherwise it would have been impracticable for the bishop to conduct every eucharistic service, as Ignatius urges and the *Apostolic Tradition* prescribes.[12]

Although dated at AD 217, the *Apostolic Tradition* attributed to Hippolytus of Rome is generally regarded as describing the situation in central Italy a generation or two earlier. There is currently a dispute among scholars as to the author, so I only use "Hippolytus" as the short generic form for whoever wrote it in Italy in his time. He or they composed it "in order that those who have been rightly instructed may hold fast to that tradition which has continued until now."[13] The book speaks of "He who is ordained as a bishop, being chosen by all the people," and

> When his name is announced and approved, the people will gather on the Lord's day with the council of elders and the bishops who are present. 3With the assent of all, the bishops will place their hands upon him, with the council of elders standing by, quietly.[14]

ELECTION BY THE LAITY

To avoid confusion about terms and for better understanding the following text, it is apropos to mention that, by the third century, the term "priest" began to designate an elder/presbyter or bishop in a monepiscopal church, and is commonly rendered such in modern Roman Catholic translations into French and English. By

11. Origen, *Hom. Ps. 81*, 7.

12. Bruce, *Spreading Flame*, 205.

13. Hippolytus, *Trad. ap.* 1.3.

14. Hippolytus, *Trad. ap.* 2.2–3.

this time period bishops, presbyters, and deacons were likened to the Levitical priesthood, or regarded as entitled to the status and perquisites of such.

Around AD 240, Origen preached that the reason for the presence of the laypeople at the ordination of a priest is to show them who the priest is and his excellent virtues, lest there later be second thoughts or remaining doubts about the priest's suitability.[15] This looks like the laity had at least a veto or right to object and stop proceedings for a particular candidate. Although he acknowledged the time-honored protocol of the church in elections by the laity just before the mass apostasy of AD 249–51, Origen criticized the conduct of congregational elections. He indicated that laity engaged in clamor and shouting. The layfolk exercised an active role with vigor, rather than passively accepting the judgment of their other leaders.

A few years later, Cyprian recorded that Cornelius was installed as bishop of Rome "by the testimony of almost all the clergy, by the suffrage of the people who were then present, and by the assembly of ancient priests and good men."[16]

In the Epistle numbered 67 in both CSEL and ANF, Cyprian noted in AD 257 that candidates for clerical office are not to be ordained without the consent of the people/laity, "especially since they themselves have the power either of choosing worthy priests, or of rejecting unworthy ones" (v. 3),[17] and:

> we observe to come from divine authority, that the priest should be chosen in the presence of the people under the eyes of all, and should be approved worthy and suitable by public judgment and testimony. (v. 4)[18]

> for the proper celebration of ordinations all the neighbouring bishops of the same province should assemble with that people for which a prelate is ordained. And the bishop should be chosen in the presence of the people,

15. Origen, *Hom. Lev.* 6.3.1.

16. Cyprian, *Ep.* 55.8.

17. CSEL 737–38.

18. CSEL 738–39.

who have most fully known the life of each one, and have
looked into the doings of each one as respects his habitual conduct. (v. 5)[19]

The last quotation illustrates that it was not the ordaining
bishops who made the choice. The bishops must by definition have
been from other parishes/dioceses, and would not have known
more than the local laity to any meaningful degree the potential
candidates, their conduct of everyday life, and habits.[20]

Some Roman Catholic scholars in our time agree that election was by the congregation rather than a supra-congregational
authority:

> One of the fundamental laws of Christianity in the first
> three centuries was that the local community, both "cler-
> gy and people", had the right to choose its own presidents
> or leaders. That right was respected by popes and was
> even confirmed by them, several times quite explicitly,
> as inviolable.[21]

> In the undivided Church of the first four centuries the
> participation of the laity, where it occurred, was con-
> sidered an integral part of the spiritual event which in-
> cluded election, ordination and reception of the newly
> ordained bishop.[22]

A PhD and Sister of Loretto, in advocating that Roman Catholic clergy be elected rather than appointed, said, "the ancient form
of selecting bishops, highly relevant in today's world. It's a method
used today—with some variations—by the Episcopal, Lutheran
and Methodist churches. It was also a method used in the first
centuries of the Christian church (before any denominations)."[23]

Another Roman Catholic source narrates: "In these early
centuries, the nominations and elections of bishops were done

19. CSEL 739–40.
20. Norton, *Episcopal Elections*, 15.
21. Huizing and Walf, *Electing Our Own Bishops*, vii.
22. Kilmartin, "Episcopal Election," 39.
23. Fiedler, "Return to Early Church Practice."

solely by a popular vote of all the faithful. Saint Cyprian believed elections prevented unworthy persons from becoming bishops."[24]

Professor Stockmeier notes: "A survey of the history of official appointments in the early Church demonstrates that bishops were undoubtedly elected by clergy and people from the beginning."[25]

However, there is the argument from Cyprian ordaining an unelected man without consulting the laity:

> to the elders and deacons, and to the whole people, greeting. In ordinations of the clergy, beloved brethren, we usually consult you beforehand, and weigh the character and deserts of individuals, with the general advice. But human testimonies must not be waited for when the divine approval precedes.[26]

On the other hand, this was not the ordination of a bishop, presbyter, or deacon. He ordained the man to be a reader, a position which was late in origin in holy orders, and was done without the laying-on of hands required for the ordinations of bishops, presbyters, and deacons.[27] It was like ordaining someone to be a sexton (janitor) or someone to take care of the chapel's public address system. The reader merely read the Scriptures at public worship, and had no official role in church government or in sacramental life.

STATUS OF CLERGY

Towards the middle of the third century, the clergy's opinion of themselves rose inversely to their spiritual decline. They magnified the importance of their offices, assumed high-sounding titles and became possessive of their authority. Origen noted that some of the higher clergy considered themselves "princes of the church."[28] In

24. Brennan, "Intriguing History," para. 2.

25. Stockmeier, "Election of Bishops," 8.

26. Cyprian, *Ep.* 32.1.

27. Hippolytus, *Trad. ap.* 11.

28. Origen, *Hom. Num.* 22.4.2, ll. 165–66; my translation of *ecclesiarum*

letters written while hiding from the Decian Persecution, Cyprian, bishop of Carthage, constantly invoked the "honour" and "dignity" of bishops, addressed other clergy as "my lord," and did not decline such honorifics when directed to himself.[29] He asserted "the Church is founded upon the bishops, and every act of the Church is controlled by these same rulers."[30] He criticized his presbyters for being insufficiently submissive to him, for acting too much on their own initiative in caring for the Carthaginian church in his absence of indefinite duration, and for not remembering "their own place."[31] This self-aggrandizement and spiritual arrogance was particularly out of place when all involved, including Cyprian himself, were in imminent danger of imprisonment, torture, and death at government hands.

With one exception, the office of apostle was regarded as having passed into history.[32] The exception is that the Didache depicts itinerant unpaid apostles, who spent only a few days in a Christian community before moving on to the next.[33] It was the same for prophets,[34] except that prophets were entitled to stay and to be fed,[35] but were otherwise not remunerated.[36] Local churches could appoint bishops and deacons as prophets.[37]

The first thirty years of the third century produced the *Didascalia*, which contains a long code of the constitutional law of the church. Although devoting eight chapters to the office of bishop, "there was no attempt to define the bishop's relation to other bishops, nor any word suggestive of a hierarchy within the episcopate,

principes in Doutreleau's edition (3:94).

29. Cyprian, *Epp.* 5–43.
30. Cyprian, *Ep.* 33.1.
31. Cyprian, *Ep.* 16.1.
32. E.g. Tertullian, *Praescr.* 44; Origen, *Hom. Isa.* 6.4.
33. Did. 11.3–6.
34. Did. 11.7–12; 13.
35. Did. 13.
36. Did. 11.8–12.
37. Did. 15.1.

whether of dignity or authority."[38] Despite its great length and exhaustive coverage of other matters of church government, it does not mention extra-congregational relations, even in passing. This is totally contrary to what we should expect in such a document, unless church polity was exclusively congregational.

PRE-CONSTANTINIAN COUNCILS ABOVE THE CONGREGATIONS?

The existence of inter-congregational synods of the ante-Nicene era does not imply that they possessed constitutional or hierarchical authority to remove a bishop/pastor from office. In the early third century, Tertullian in Tunisia wrote that Christians in Greece held councils among the churches at which "all the deeper questions are handled for the common benefit" and "the actual representation of the whole Christian name is celebrated."[39] Whatever the universality claimed for such synods, Tertullian refers to them as being found mostly or only in the Aegean area.[40] Some of them considered the issue of what constituted the canon of Scripture,[41] such as the Shepherd of Hermas, with no final consensus. It is true that Epistle 75.4 in the Cyprianic collection mentions that in Cappadocia at the time of the Rebaptism Controversy, "it happens of necessity among us, that year by year we, the elders and prelates, assemble together to arrange those matters which are committed to our care, so that if any things are more serious they may be directed by the common counsel,"[42] but this speaks of presbyters and an undefined class of church officers, and even then for consultation rather than binding legislation or church discipline. The word here translated "prelates" is not *praelati* with its modern redolence of high ecclesiastical governance like a bishop, but

---

38. Connolly, *Didascalia Apostolorum*, xxxviii.

39. Tertullian, *Jejun.* 13.

40. Kretschmar, "Councils of the Ancient Church," 6; Tertullian, *Jejun.* 13.

41. Tertullian, *Pud.* 10.

42. Firmilian, *Ep. Cypriano* 4.

praepositi, which denotes leaders of any sort. In fact, the thrust of this Epistle was that the bishop of Rome was not a higher officer over all other bishops and could intervene in local bishoprics. *Praepositus* also appears in Cyprian's *Epistle* 3.3, where he writes that, as far as deacons are concerned, *praepositi* and bishops are successors of the apostles,[43] thus distinguishing between their office and that of bishops. An Oxford doctoral thesis translates it as "those in charge."[44] His Epistle 67 speaks of the people for whom a *praepositus* is to be ordained bishop, not that the man was already a bishop.

According to Irenaeus, religious disputes which could not be resolved within a single congregation were to be taken to "the most ancient Churches with which the apostles held constant intercourse, and learn from them what is certain and clear in regard to the present question," rather than through a hierarchy of diocesan bishops, metropolitans, presbyteries, or regional councils.[45]

A number of disputes arose in the first three centuries of Christian writings, which would have warranted a universal or at least regional authority over more than one congregation to settle: (1) against the Montanists, (2) during the Paschal Controversy, (3) councils with Origen in Arabia, and (4) on the rebaptism of converts from non-catholic Christian denominations. However, no council intervened in a congregation or disciplined a bishop. In reality, they were no more than rallies to ventilate solidarity. The same instances also witness that there was no metropolitan or other diocesan bishop to settle the differences.

(1) During the Montanist Controversy of the late second century, the bishops of two provinces neighboring on Phrygia met, investigated, condemned the Montanists as heretical, and purported to excommunicate them.[46] Our records of these synods do not indicate that such assemblies were organs of church government above the congregations or their bishops, because (a) the synods

43. Apostolos id est episcopos et praepositos Dominus elegit.
44. Norton, *Episcopal Elections*, 12.
45. Irenaeus, *Haere.* 3.4.1.
46. Apolinaris of Hierapolis, *Letter to Abircius Marcellus.*

were held in different provinces from the one where the excommunications were to take effect even though there were plenty of non-Montanist Christians in Phrygia, (b) the extant records do not indicate whether they were cast out of the church by the Phrygian congregations themselves, and (c) they were ad hoc in timing, not in perpetual session nor scheduled to recur at fixed intervals.

(2) In the AD 180s, a dispute came to a head over the proper day to end the Lenten fast and celebrate Easter. During this Paschal or Quartodeciman Controversy, Bishop Victor of Rome circulated letters on his own authority denouncing the opposite view and tried to excommunicate all its supporters, especially the ones in western Anatolia. Each side held synods and conferences of bishops, unanimously passing resolutions in favor of their own practice.[47] An examination of the circumstances reveals that these councils were not levels of ecclesiastical government with authority to intervene in a congregation by enforcing a decision or adjudicating its internal differences. Their habitual unanimity more than suggests that they did not come together as continuing forums of recognized jurisdiction, but as voluntary self-assembled rallies of adherents of a particular position. Moreover, Irenaeus and other bishops in Victor's party very firmly rebuked him over the intended excommunications.[48] In any event, the two sides came to a compromise whereby both groups tolerated the practice of each other, an accord[49] which lasted over a century. Given these circumstances, especially the compromise, none of these synods could hardly have regarded themselves as authoritative over any but their local church, nor Victor as paramount bishop (pope).

(3) Half a century later, there were two gatherings of clergy in Arabia in response to the suspected heresy of Bishop Beryllus of Bostra and Bishop Heracleides and other bishops with them. The method of proceeding was that Origen and the suspect bishops discussed the issue in the presence of a church assembly. He was

47. Eusebius, *Church History* 5.23.

48. Eusebius, *Church History* 5.24.

49. Eusebius, *Church History* 5.24.11–18; Anatolius of Laodicea, *Paschal Canon* 10.

persuasive and knowledgeable and they were open-minded, with the result that they freely changed their minds. Nobody coerced or threatened the bishops. It would be sheer speculation to say what either assembly might have done if Origen had failed to convince. For all this, the laity possessed a right to confirm or reject the decisions accepted by their bishops.[50]

(4) When Novatianists and other Christians who were converted from other Christian denominations applied for admission to the mainline church, the Catholics themselves divided over whether baptism by schismatic or heretical clergy was void as having been administered by ministers without any status as Christians or as a church.[51] Cyprian of Carthage led one party, Stephen of Rome the other. Both convened large gatherings which upheld their respective positions.[52] For instance, a synod of eighty-seven bishops assembled at Carthage under the presidency of Cyprian in AD 256 unanimously endorsed his views. Such amazing uniformity of judgment in the face of similar unanimity to the contrary at meetings for the other side reinforces the suspicion that the councils were attended voluntarily and only by the likeminded.

Cyprian participated in other councils in his part of northern Africa, concerning such issues as clergymen as executors under a Will,[53] Novatianism,[54] infant baptism,[55] and Christians who had apostatized during the Decian Persecution and sought reinstatement in the church,[56] and the rebaptism of heretics.[57] Such councils were with other bishops, for which he probably also used the synonym "priests." He also held a council attended by "bishops, presbyters, deacons, and confessors, as well as with the laity,"[58] but

50. Origen, *Dial.* 6.8–10.

51. Cyprian, *Epp.* 70–74.

52. Dionysius of Alexandria, *Letter to Sextus II of Rome.*

53. Cyprian, *Ep.* 1.

54. Cyprian, *Ep.* 55.

55. Cyprian, *Ep.* 64.

56. Cyprian, *Epp.* 55–57, 64, 67.

57. Cyprian, *Ep.* 73.

58. Cyprian, *Ep.* 30.5.

this was probably a regular congregational meeting in contrast to the others, with these others sometimes including forty, fifty, sixty, or more bishops. Others of his letters disclose only that a council was held and its subject matter. All such synods appear to be ad hoc rather than scheduled to recur at set intervals. They show a trend in church life that synods became more frequent, and that they were becoming relied upon as persuasive in addition to scripture and tradition.

There is little information about a "Council of Lambese" or other synods which dealt with Privatus. Our sources[59] do not state that he was a bishop. Moreover, they indicate that Privatus and his party posed a threat to episcopal security of tenure, for they conspired to appoint rival bishops in place of those already in office.

On the contrary, three other instances affirmatively demonstrate that there was no authority over the congregation to settle or even mediate internal disputes, such as schism:

(1) In the second decade of the third century, the church at Rome split into two factions, one of which elected Hippolytus as bishop. The schism continued until a voluntary reconciliation in AD 235. Although Christians outside the territory of the bishop of Rome, such as Tertullian, gave moral support to one side or the other,[60] not even neighboring congregations intervened to heal the rift by removing the one who was not the rightful bishop or otherwise facilitating a settlement. The implication is that they lacked authority to do so.

(2) While still a layman based in Egypt, Origen often traveled as a theological consultant to churches throughout the Near East. When pausing in Palestine in AD 219 he was ordained a presbyter by the bishops of Caesarea and Jerusalem. This brought protests from his own bishop, Demetrius of Alexandria. A decade later, while Origen was in the process of moving permanently to Palestine, Demetrius summoned a council of his clergy, which dismissed him as a professor in the Alexandrian theological school and excommunicated him. Later, Demetrius convoked a second

59. Cyprian, *Ep.* 36.4; Hefele, *History of the Christian Councils*, 90–91.

60. Frend, *Rise of Christianity*, 350–51.

assembly which deprived him of the status of elder. Those synods are not evidence that ante-Nicene bishops could be removed from office, for Origen was not a monepiscopal bishop but only a presbyter in an era when the two offices had become quite distinct and elders held very low status. Nor is the second council an indication that presbyters could be demoted to lay status, for its decision was not recognized by the churches in Greece, Lebanon, Arabia, or, most significantly, Palestine.[61] It was in Palestine that Origen's controversial ordination had been performed and where he spent the rest of his life: the decrees of the Alexandrian synods were not in force in the very place where they could have consequence. Moreover, the second assembly can have been no more than a collective display of hostility, because it is impossible to understand how the second assembly could regard him as an officer of the church after the first synod had declared him to be no longer a member of it. Purporting to deprive a person of status of an official is a tacit admission that he held such office in the first place. The lack of central authority in the universal church was also demonstrated by Origen in AD 246: to reverse his excommunication, he wrote not only to the bishop of Rome, but to all the bishops who had ratified it.[62]

(3) Sharp differences came to a head in AD 251 when a faction in the church at Rome accepted Novatian as its bishop in rivalry to Cornelius, thus repeating Hippolytus's situation of a generation or two earlier. Churches outside Rome took sides, and Cornelius and Novatian ordained competing bishops for congregations throughout the Roman Empire. Cornelius's party did not seek to conduct judicial proceedings or to discipline Novatianist bishops, but declared that their ordinations were invalid from the beginning, i.e., that they had never been bishops at all.[63] The non-Novatianists later fell out among themselves over whether the Novatianists had completely left the Christian church.[64] Naturally, a person cannot

---

61. Jerome, *Ep.* 33.4; Quasten, *Patrology*, 2:39.

62. Bigg, *Christian Platonists of Alexandria*, 258–59.

63. Cyprian, *Epp.* 44.1; 55.24; Eusebius, *Church History* 6.43.

64. Cyprian, *Epp.* 44; 45.3; 47; 50; 52; 55; 68; 73.2; 74; 75.

hold office in an organization of which he is no longer a member nor fill an office unless he has been duly elected or appointed. This was not an instance of a bishop refusing to abide by the decision of a properly-constituted supervisory body, but of separate and competing denominations. It is also to be noted that the argument of Cornelius's faction turned on the validity and priority of ordinations and harmony with other bishops,[65] not how Novatianist bishops treated their flocks. Even so, the remaining churchmen disagreed among themselves as to whether Novatianist baptism was valid.

One letter of Cyprian discloses that there were other assemblies of clergy to deliberate on both what to do with Christians who had lapsed during the Decian Persecution and what to do about the Novatianists, but they did not indicate that their decisions were binding on bishops or congregations that did not agree.[66] As in the Paschal (Quartodeciman) Controversy, these inter-congregational conventions were mere partisan rallies, with effects only on the morale of their adherents.

(4) In poverty when he began his clerical career, Paul of Samosata amassed a fortune as bishop of Antioch through blackmail, bribes, and plundering the church. He also turned his parish into a personality cult. He brought Christianity into disrepute by adopting the title, affectations, and pomp of a high secular official in an era when many Christians considered the secular power an agency of Satan. He compelled the laity to applaud his sermons, denigrated his predecessors, lived luxuriously, preached while intoxicated, kept mistresses, and maintained choirs to sing his praise. There was no open opposition among his elders or deacons, and the laity acquiesced in his excesses. In AD 268 a large assembly of bishops from other congregations purported to depose and excommunicate him, but it appears that they did so because of his heretical Christology, not for or not primarily for these excesses.[67] Paul refused to hand over the church premises, and his administration

---

65. Cyprian, *Epp.* 55.8, 24.

66. Cyprian, *Ep.* 55.3; Ware, "Patterns of Episcopacy," 17–18.

67. Eusebius, *Church History* 7.28–30.

remained intact. He left office only after the civil government intervened, after he had sided with an unsuccessful enemy of Rome in a war. After the war, the emperor felt it necessary to restore Roman control of the church as well as the state.[68] That Paul could engage in such activities for a long period without effective opposition indicates an ironclad deference to the autonomy of the congregation, and the absence of any accepted ecclesiastical system of deposing an unsatisfactory bishop by church authorities from outside it. The eventual deposition was effected by the (pagan) secular government.

In his opening discourse at the Council of Carthage in 256, Cyprian denied that there was any hierarchy among bishops or any churchmen superior to a bishop:

> neither does any of us set himself up as a bishop of bishops, nor by tyrannical terror does any compel his colleague to the necessity of obedience; since every bishop, according to the allowance of his liberty and power, has his own proper right of judgment, and can no more be judged by another than he himself can judge another. But let us all wait for the judgment of our Lord Jesus Christ.[69]

In actual practice, Cyprian acted as leader of the Catholic Church in the Province of Africa[70] and some other parts of the western Mediterranean world. He worked from personal charisma with the consent of his equals, acting almost from the force of events. All the while, he never claimed primacy for himself, and denied it for Bishop Stephen of Rome. His leadership began after the devastating epidemic and mass apostasy of AD 249–51, which killed off many leading believers, opening opportunities to make other changes in Christianity. In the same era, according to Georg Kretschmar, "Cyprian's theology of church office . . . corresponded to an ecclesiastical structure that was not limited to Africa: the

---

68. Grant, *Augustus to Constantine*, 218.

69. ANF 5:565.

70. LeBreton and Zeiller, *History of the Primitive Church*, 2:1120.

coexistence of individual congregations, usually not large, which were also actually independent of one another."[71]

In the early AD 250s Cornelius of Rome mentioned to Fabius of Antioch that the church at Rome included forty-six presbyters, seven deacons, and seven sub-deacons. It could be argued that these numbers imply there were several centers of Christian activity under his jurisdiction distributed throughout the countryside, including worship, for it is hard to conceive all of them were contained on a single church campus. They would thus appear to be heads of congregations, making Cornelius a diocesan bishop.[72] However, in the time of Justinian the staff of Hagia Sophia, or at least the city of Constantinople, included sixty priests, one hundred deacons, and ninety sub-deacons,[73] which would show the number of priests or presbyters in early city churches could be much greater than today.

No Christian writer in this era criticized other Christians on the issue of the structure(s) or hierarchy(ies) in which congregations or office-bearers of the church were organized. The nearest to an exception is Tertullian, who faulted heretical denominations for the carelessness and nonchalance in promoting and rotating church officers, but he did not criticize their governmental structure itself.[74] First Clement's complaint was similar: it opposed the unjustified exchange of elders and deacons within the congregational structure, but not the constitutional polity of the Corinthians. There was liberty in how a congregation organized itself, so long as there was continuity, stability, and no violence involved.

71. Kretschmar, "Councils of the Ancient Church," 14–15.

72. Eusebius, *Church History* 6.43.11.

73. Norton, *Episcopal Elections*, 69; Kostash, "Once There Were Deaconesses."

74. Tertullian, *Praescr.* 41.

CHAPTER 3

Beginning of Transition from Congregational to Diocesan Bishops

IN THE FOURTH CENTURY, CHRISTIANITY was a major force in the world, and still is in some quarters. Near its beginning, however, it was met by a force that was stronger at the time, and shaped its structure in a way that persists to the present day in denominations such as the Eastern Orthodox, Oriental Orthodox, Episcopalian and, in an extended form, the Roman Catholic. The previous chapter showed that in the second and third centuries church polity was congregational, with local assemblies being independent of outside ecclesiastical authorities, for instance in the choice of its officers. Later, the influence of the Roman emperors solidified a new form of polity in which congregations were no longer autonomous. Although there was a long period of mixed structures, we can trace the beginnings or solidification of diocesan episcopacy to Constantine the Great, both before and after he became emperor.

CONSTANTINE

The Peace of the Church reveals the beginning of the transition from single autonomous congregations, or congregations with a few campuses, being replaced by a hierarchy over many congregations, and was probably its cause. Constantine wanted a centralized, or at least unified and tidy, organization to make this aspect of the empire easier to govern, and making it a unifying force of his rule.

From the beginning, Constantine intervened in church affairs, with the purpose of keeping it in peace and unity. He convened a few synods before and after the First Council of Nicaea,[1] and called and presided at this first ecumenical council. He also judged theological and personal disputes between Christians directly.[2] According to Eusebius,

> he exercised a peculiar care over the church of God: and whereas, in the several provinces there were some who differed from each other in judgment, he, like some general bishop constituted by God, convened synods of his ministers. Nor did he disdain to be present and sit with them in their assembly, but bore a share in their deliberations, ministering to all that pertained to the peace of God.[3]

> He likewise added the sanction of his authority to the decisions of bishops passed at their synods, and forbade the provincial governors to annul any of their decrees: for he rated the priests of God at a higher value than any judge whatever.[4]

Constantine's first reaction to the Arian Controversy was to send a mediator[5] and wrote letters to the parties urging them to end it, and telling them the subject of dispute was an insignificant matter,[6] pleading for them to end the dissension.[7]

---

1. Barnes, *Constantine and Eusebius*, 228–29, 235–36, 238, 266.
2. Barnes, *Constantine and Eusebius*, 232–33, 238–40, 242.
3. Eusebius, *Vit. Const.* 1.44.
4. Eusebius, *Vit. Const.* 4.27.
5. Eusebius, *Vit. Const.* 2.63.
6. Eusebius, *Vit. Const.* 2.63–72.
7. Eusebius, *Vit. Const.* 2.64–72.

In his opening address to the Council of Nicaea, he opined that

> in my judgment, intestine strife within the Church of God, is far more evil and dangerous than any kind of war or conflict; and these our differences appear to me more grievous than any outward trouble. . . . I feel that my desires will be most completely fulfilled when I can see you all united in one judgment, and that common spirit of peace and concord prevailing amongst you all,[8]

During the Nicene Council's deliberations,

> he appeared in a truly attractive and amiable light, persuading some, convincing others by his reasonings, praising those who spoke well, and urging all to unity of sentiment, until at last he succeeded in bringing them to one mind and judgment respecting every disputed question.[9]

This was in keeping with his belief that he was the chief and paramount officer of the church:

> On the occasion of his entertaining a company of bishops, he let fall the expression, "that he himself too was a bishop," addressing them in my hearing in the following words: "You are bishops whose jurisdiction is within the Church: I also am a bishop, ordained by God to overlook whatever is external to the Church." And truly his measures corresponded with his words: for he watched over his subjects with an episcopal care.[10]

A little later, he intervened in the election of a bishop for Antioch, to end dissention and restore harmony,[11] and wrote to a synod at Tyre that it end dissentions.[12] He banned heretical and

---

8. Eusebius, *Vit. Const.* 3.12.
9. Eusebius, *Vit. Const.* 3.13.
10. Eusebius, *Vit. Const.* 4.24.
11. Eusebius, *Vit. Const.* 3.59–72.
12. Eusebius, *Vit. Const.* 4.42.

schismatic assemblies, and gave their church buildings to the Catholics.[13]

In short, Constantine's reign saw an amalgamation of church and state in his person, or as at least tended towards it.[14] Eusebius's *Panegyric to Constantine* says, "invested as he is with a semblance of heavenly sovereignty, he directs his gaze above, and frames his earthly government according to the pattern of that Divine original, feeling strength in its conformity to the monarchy of God,"[15] and "two mighty powers, starting from the same point, the Roman empire, which henceforth was swayed by a single sovereign, and the Christian religion, subdued and reconciled these contending elements."[16] The desired polity could not be congregational, for this was out of keeping with the sentiment of a leading churchman of the day that "surely monarchy far transcends every other constitution and form of government: for that democratic equality of power, which is its opposite, may rather be described as anarchy and disorder."[17] As a lifelong soldier and the son of a prominent general, Constantine was well acquainted with stratification into ranks, so it was only natural that he would use the military model for the Catholic Church as well.

Constantine advised one of his successors as emperor that it would avail him nothing to be possessed of imperial power, unless he could establish uniformity of worship throughout his empire.[18] In the same official vein, Constantine "appointed Christians to be governors of the provinces, ordering honour to be shown to the [Christian] priests, and threatening with death those who dared to insult them."[19] Government approval or even the threat of force in instituting diocesan episcopacy would also reduce or convert opposition to the new polity. The alternative was for the Emperor

---

13. Eusebius, *Vit. Const.* 3.64–65.
14. Frend, *Early Church*, 150.
15. Eusebius, *Laud. Const.* 3.5.
16. Eusebius, *Laud. Const.* 16.5.
17. Eusebius, *Laud. Const.* 3.6.
18. Sozomen, *Ecclesiastical History* 3.19.
19. Theodoret, *Hist. eccl.* 1.1.

to be personally approached by everyone who had a grievance with the local bishop; later emperors expressed disapproval of such manner of independent appeals. In addition, the wholesale conversions to Christianity and rise in the number of laity during his reign necessitated a structure of governance different from one designed for a few congregations of far fewer members, so few that the apostle Paul could address their members by name in his epistles.

A hierarchical clergy was an administrative necessity for the emperors. Through providing salaries and other benefits to the clergy and exempting them from various secular duties, Constantine and his successors had made them government servants. To keep order and ensure efficiency, these bureaucrats needed to be governed and regulated, in a way similar to that of the secular administrators. The most obvious way to control the front line in this new department of government was to confer powers of supervision and discipline on diocesan and metropolitan bishops. Such a hierarchical arrangement, culminating in the emperor, would provide efficiency and minimize conflict in the church, leaving the emperors more time for other branches of their government. So also, the imperial policy and efforts for the unity of the church: no organization can tolerate rival bureaucracies, or independent action, without a common overriding supervisor.

The relatively new office of metropolitan, first mentioned during Constantine's reign, was an innovation very useful in administration of the church and empire from the top down. The emperor need not be bothered by appeals directly from the parties in the lower dioceses and could influence the choice of their bishops, as long as he appointed the "right" men as metropolitans, who could veto candidates for bishoprics that would not fit in with the imperial designs.[20]

20. Norton, *Episcopal Elections*, 82, 109.

COUNCILS AMONG BISHOPS

The first extra-congregational provisions to prescribe for the supervision and deposition of clergy began at the Council or Synod
of Elvira. Fifteen to twenty years before Nicaea, but de facto after the Diocletian Persecution, nineteen bishops and twenty-six
presbyters from far southern and southeastern Spain assembled.[21]
Among them was Bishop Hosius of Cordova, who later became
a close advisor of the Emperor Constantine and leading figure at
the First Council of Nicaea. The Canons of Elvira prescribe that a
bishop is to be deposed from office for practicing usury (Canon
20), for sexual intercourse with his wife (33), for receiving back
into communion a Christian who has been excommunicated by
another bishop (53), and for certain sins committed before ordination (30, 51, 76). The last three are also bars to ordination in
the first place. In comparison, the usual penalties for laymen and
laywomen were suspensions from Holy Communion for various
lengths of times, which contrast with deposition from office and
other, stricter, provisions against clergy. The Council removed
leaders that their congregations had put in place, but did not yet
purport to elect new clergy.

Although Elvira preceded the *Edict of Milan*, it nevertheless
took place during the beginnings of peace and toleration for the
church, because the Diocletian Persecution was little enforced
Spain or elsewhere in the western empire.[22] The emperors there,
Constantine and his father, were tolerant of Christianity and gave
the laws against Christianity only slight enforcement.[23] For instance, at the city of Rome the persecution of Christians ended in

21. For the date of the Council of Elvira, see Lane Fox, *Pagans and Chris-
tians*, 664–66, and Evans Grubbs, "'Pagan' and 'Christian' Marriage," 399n156.
Barnes, *Constantine and Eusebius*, 53, dates Elvira as prior to the Diocletian
Persecution.

22. Barnes, *Constantine and Eusebius*, 28, 38, 54; Southern, *Roman Empire
from Severus to Constantine*, 280–81.

23. Barnes, *Constantine and Eusebius*, 28–29; Eusebius, *Vit. Const.* 1.13,
16; Grant, *Augustus to Constantine*, 230–31; Southern, *Roman Empire from
Severus to Constantine*, 168.

AD 305.[24] Besides the relief of the church in the West granted by Constantine and his family and the other Western Emperor,[25] the co-emperor Galerius officially ended the Persecution in the East in AD 311.[26] The Constantinian dynasty's toleration and participation in the church show that they took a favorable view of the Christian faith, and sought to provide stability and peace, which would materially aid in its progress. Emperors in this dynasty sponsored other synods or councils of bishops with a view to ending discontent in the church and keeping it united.

The events giving rise to the Council of Arles warrant special attention. In AD 312 two factions at Carthage separately elected its own bishop. They refused to recognize each other's ordination. The Donatists, the party which held the later election, argued that the first ordination was invalid because it had not been performed by the mandatory quorum of three bishops. There had indeed been three consecrators, but one of them was alleged to have apostatized by cooperating with the pagan government during a persecution, an agency of Satan, and thus put himself outside the church. Their theory was that a cleric tainted with a history of apostasy forfeited any authority he might have in the church, including capacity to ordain. This alienation from the faith infected all who traced church status through him. Lines of ordination descended from him were nullities. Christians elsewhere in north Africa took sides, with rival bishops and competing congregations soon lining the coast. Then the Donatists appealed to the Emperor Constantine, who wished to see Christianity prosper without dissension.[27] His Imperial Majesty appointed an arbitration panel, which met at the Lateran in AD 313. It decided against the Donatists, but recognized their ordinations, with the proviso that where a bishopric had more than one claimant, the one ordained later must yield to the earlier, and find another parish.[28] This proviso included Car-

24. Grant, *Augustus to Constantine*, 186.
25. Southern, *Roman Empire from Severus to Constantine*, 168.
26. Southern, *Roman Empire from Severus to Constantine*, 280–81.
27. Barnes, *Constantine and Eusebius*, 57–58, 212.
28. Barnes, *Constantine and Eusebius*, 57.

thage itself, thus setting aside the election of the Donatist who had engendered the controversy. Ordinations, even of dissidents, were upheld on the criteria of priority of election and the technicalities of the consecration procedure.[29] The Donatists refused to accept this decision and again appealed to the emperor, who then ordered a second synod to meet at Arles. It agreed with the Lateran decision, deciding on the basis of formal procedures in the ordination process, not on substantive issues of honesty or conduct in office.[30] In 315 there was yet another appeal, which Constantine decided in person.[31] Such appeals to and reliance on the secular power would have been unthinkable during the persecutions.[32]

The attendance at Arles in AD 314 indicates that Christian clergy could move freely throughout the western Empire, with bishops or their representatives coming from Britain, Dalmatia, Gaul, Mauretania, Numidia, Sardinia, Sicily, mainland Italy, Spain, and Tunisia, without molestation by the government as happened during the long history of persecutions.

The control of congregations from outside, which was believed would end disunity and complete Constantine's efforts to make the Catholic Church an efficient, hierarchical, bureaucracy, seemingly came at the First Council of Nicaea (AD 325). Its fourth Canon decreed:

> It is by all means proper that a bishop should be appointed by all the bishops in the province; but should this be difficult, either on account of urgent necessity or because of distance, three at least should meet together, and the suffrages of the absent [bishops] also being given and communicated in writing, then the ordination should take place. But in every province the ratification of what is done should be left to the Metropolitan.[33]

---

29. Frend, *Donatist Church*, 149.

30. Frend, *Donatist Church*, 146–50.

31. Barnes, *Constantine and Eusebius*, 59–60

32. Grant, *Augustus to Constantine*, 237–38; Frend, *Donatist Church*, 147.

33. First Council of Nicaea, Canon 4.

Canon 4 was reinforced by Canons 12 and 13 of the Synod of Laodicea (AD 363–64): "Bishops are to be appointed to the ecclesiastical government by the judgment of the metropolitans and neighboring bishops," and "The election of those who are to be appointed to the priesthood is not to be committed to the multitude."[34] However, the word here translated "multitude" (ὄχλος) is not the usual word for "people" (λαος, δημος) in reference to an election, but signifies a tumult or mob, which intimidates sincere voters.[35] An earlier post-Constantinian council ruled that the combined consent of the laity and of the candidate for bishop was insufficient; it was also necessary that he be approved by a full synod, including the metropolitan.[36]

The history and usage of the church in the century after Nicaea would indicate that the role of the bishops in Canon 4 was confined to a mere monopoly of the ordination ceremony by laying-on of hands of candidates after nomination and approval by the laity over whom he was to be bishop. In practice, incumbent bishops did not exercise the sole right to appoint bishops, but merely possessed a veto by not participating in the ordination rite. A similar veto is given the metropolitan. Historians for the century after the Council record far too many appointments by laity for the canons to have any additional force. On the other hand, unilateral appointment from outside does emerge as the fourth century progressed.

34. Synod of Laodicea, Canons 12–13.
35. Norton, *Episcopal Elections*, 44–45; Synod of Laodicea, Canons 12–13.
36. Council of Antioch *in Encaeniis*, Canon 16.

CHAPTER 4

Church Government
in the Fourth Century

I TAKE MUCH OF THE following information from three church historians who wrote in the early fifth century who envisioned their work to be a continuation of Eusebius's *Church History*. The first, Socrates Scholasticus, also known as Socrates of Constantinople, covers the church from AD 305 to 439. The extant text of Sozomen dates from AD 440 or 443, and describes it from the second century onwards. Although three-quarters of the book depends on Socrates, it is a new work in which he added material from other sources and went back to the sources from which the earlier writer drew. Theodoret's history ends at AD 429, although it was completed two decades later, and contains material from sources other than Socrates and Sozomen. Theodoret was a bishop who was well-educated in ecclesiastical history. In the interests of brevity, and to avoid unnecessary duplication, the title *Ecclesiastical History*, the title of all three, is omitted from the footnote entries for Socrates Scholasticus, Sozomen, and Theodoret.

The most usual pattern described by the three historians was for a bishop to be designated as over a single city.[1] On the other

---

1. Socrates Scholasticus 1.11, 12; 2.37; 3.5, 10; 4.11, 26; 6.11, 17, 22;

hand, both Sozomen and Theodoret record exceptions that tend to indicate that at least some bishops were diocesan rather than of a single congregation or city, as the following demonstrates.

Some men called "bishops" appear to have been metropolitans over other bishops, or diocesan bishops over congregational ones. Theodoret 5.4 states that one bishop of Tarsus had jurisdiction over all Cilicians which would appear to include supervision over the bishops of Mopsuestia[2] and Neronias,[3] Theodoret 2.12 mentions a bishop of the metropolis of Gaul and a bishop of the metropolis of the Isles of Sardinia. It mentions both a bishop of the metropolis of Italy and the bishop of Rome in the same list. All these provinces also possessed bishops over various towns and cities.

Sozomen specifically uses the word "metropolitan" for some bishops: "When Cyril was first installed in the bishopric of Jerusalem, he had a dispute with Acacius, bishop of Cæsarea, concerning his rights as a Metropolitan, which he claimed on the ground of his bishopric being an apostolic see."[4] In a parallel context is "Epiphanius was at this period at the head of the metropolitan church of Cyprus."[5]

SOME BISHOPRICS CALL FOR SPECIAL ATTENTION:

Alexandria, Egypt

One of the issues at the Council of Nicaea was how to deal with Meletius, a bishop in Upper Egypt, who had ordained clergy in Alexandria while its bishop was unavailable due to the Diocletian

---

Sozomen 3.16; 6.21, 34; 8.2.

2. Theodoret 5.27, 39.
3. Theodoret 1.6; 2.6.
4. Sozomen 4.25.
5. Sozomen 7.27.

Persecution. The duties of the officers he ordained included visiting the unfortunate and caring for them as Christian priests[6]—the sort of work we would consider characteristic of parish pastors. This indicates the bishop of Alexandria was a diocesan bishop leading many parishes, with other clergy under him.

> It was the custom in Alexandria, as it still is in the present day, that all the churches should be under one bishop, but that each presbyter should have his own church, in which to assemble the people. . . .
>
> Mareotes is a district of Alexandria; there are contained in it very many villages, and an abundant population, with numerous splendid churches; these churches are all under the jurisdiction of the bishop of Alexandria, and are subject to his city as parishes.[7]

In describing a later period, Sozomen 8.14 speaks of Theophilus, Bishop of Alexandria "with the concurrence of the bishops under his jurisdiction," indicating that Theophilus was some sort of bishop of bishops, perhaps meaning that he was a diocesan bishop over many clerics who were in turn bishops in the older sense of overseers over a single congregation each, but more likely that he was a metropolitan over a group of diocesan bishops.

Rome

Socrates 4.12 describes Liberius, who is known from other passages in the three historians, as "bishop of Italy," while Theodoret 2.12 titles him "bishop of Rome" and calls a certain Dionysius, "bishop of the metropolis of Italy."

---

6. Phileas of Thmuis, *To Meletius*; Peter of Alexandria, *Letter to the Church at Alexandria*.

7. Socrates Scholasticus 1.15, 27.

Mesopotamia

Socrates Scholasticus 6.15, 6.19, and 7.8 uniformly speak of Mesopotamia having only one bishop, named Manuthas. Yet at 1.22 he mentions that Archelaus was bishop of Caschara, one of the cities of Mesopotamia. Archelaus was the orthodox protagonist in a book entitled *The Disputation of Archelaus Bishop of Caschara*. Caschara or ancient Carrhae was a major ancient city in Upper Mesopotamia. From listing two bishops over Upper Mesopotamia, it would appear that (1) Caschara was later incorporated in or expanded to the whole of Mesopotamia, or (2) the bishopric of Cashara was a parish having its own bishop in the first-century sense who was subject to Manuthas as diocesan bishop over several such, and Archelaus was a parish pastor of a congregation, or (3) Manuthas was higher still, a metropolitan.

In *The Acts of the Disputation with the Heresiarch Manes*, Diodorus the presbyter wrote to Archelaus the bishop about a new heretic (Manes) arriving in his town. They sent letters to each other, which indicates they were a considerable distance apart, about three to five days' journey, rather than speaking orally. Yet Archelaus exercised a preaching and teaching ministry in Diodorus's town, which could imply that he possessed some sort of ecclesiastical authority there, which argues for some species of diocesan episcopacy in the area of Syria between the times of Cyprian and the Nicene Council. There would be a presbyter of a parish, and a bishop of a diocese.

However, the context renders this conclusion doubtful. Manes's first contact with Archelaus was by sending a letter to a Christian in the place where Archelaus incontrovertibly was bishop. Archelaus converted the bearer of the letter to orthodox Christianity, and thus Archelaus had at his disposal for some time a resident expert on Manicheism who resided with or near him. "Neither did he omit any opportunity of conversing with Archelaus the bishop. For both these parties were very diligently engaged in investigating the practices of Manichaeus."[8] In short, Archelaus

8. Archelaus, *Disp.* 6.

was well-versed in Manes's doctrine before he met him, which was even longer than Manes's contact with Diodorus. In his own town or city, Archelaus had debated Manes in front of a large audience twenty-seven chapters before Diodorus is mentioned. For this debate Archelaus received "many tokens of honour."[9]

Diodorus probably called on Archelaus only because he considered him the best-qualified Christian for his own debate with Manes, rather than because his bishopric included Diodorus's town. In his first letter, Diodorus told Archelaus "I have heard that you have studied such matters in no ordinary degree,"[10] and "the learning which I possess for the discussion of themes like these does not meet the requirements of my desire and purpose."[11] At the debate in the town of Diodorus, Archelaus himself said "I now take the place of Diodorus, not on account of any impossibilities attaching to him, but because I came to know this person here at a previous time, when he made his way with his wicked designs into the parts where I reside."[12] It was like the theologians at Vatican II: Diodorus called on Archelaus because he was an expert in the field and had studied it more thoroughly, rather than as possessing superior ecclesiastical jurisdiction, oversight, and command over the clergy in Diodorus's town.

Although Archelaus appears in Jerome's *De Viris Illustribus* 72 and on the internet, I cannot find him in Quasten or Eusebius's *Church History*, nor indexed in the *Encyclopedia of Early Christianity*.[13] Jerome dates him to the reign of Probus (AD 276–82). This would place the events giving rise to the *Disputation* as early as AD 278, but W. H. C. Frend,[14] and the said *Encyclopedia* under "Hegemonius," believe it is fourth century. Chapter 27 of the *Disputation* itself states that it took place "well-nigh three hundred years after" the apostles were commissioned, or fourth century. Socrates

---

9. Archelaus, *Disp.* 39.

10. Archelaus, *Disp.* 40.

11. Archelaus, *Disp.* 40.

12. Archelaus, *Disp.* 46.

13. See Ferguson, *Encyclopedia of Early Christianity*.

14. Frend, *Rise of Christianity*, 386.

Scholasticus 1.22 mentions it among accounts pertaining to the lifetime of Constantine; Sozomen and Theoderet are silent. Given the uncertainties over its date, the facts in the *Disputation* render it of doubtful value in any inference of a bishop exercising jurisdiction over more than one city before the reign of Constantine.

Scythia

Sozomen 6.21 attributes the firmness in their faith of Christians of the large and populous country of Scythia, with many cities and villages, to the circumstance that it was ruled by only one bishop.[15] Note that the Scythians did not become subjects of the Roman Empire until Constantine conquered them.[16] No representative from Scythia at the Council of Nicaea is mentioned in Cowper's lists.[17] From this it can be concluded that they were poorly acquainted with ante-Nicene ecclesiastical church structures, and would have assumed that hierarchical episcopacy was an inalienable part of Christianity.

Cyprus

Socrates Scholasticus 1.12 mentions a bishop of one of the cities in Cyprus named Trimithus, while in 1.8 and 1.12 Spyridon is the bishop of one of the cities in Cyprus. In 6.10 Epiphanius is designated the bishop of Constantia in Cyprus, and 6.10 also mentions a synod of the bishops in Cyprus. On the other hand are "Spyridon, bishop of Cyprus,"[18] and he had "been assigned the bishopric of one of the cities in Cyprus."[19] Socrates refers to a successor as "Epiphanius bishop of Constantia in Cyprus,"[20] while his 5.24 has

15. Also Theodoret 4.31 as to "all the cities."
16. Eusebius, *Vit. Const.* 4:5.
17. Cowper, *Syriac Miscellanies.*
18. Socrates Scholasticus 1.8.
19. Socrates Scholasticus 1.12.
20. Socrates Scholasticus 6.10.

"Epiphanius, bishop of Cyprus."[21] Sozomen 7.27 says "Epiphanius was at this period at the head of the metropolitan church of Cyprus." Theodoret does not mention Epiphanius or any clergy of or in Cyprus.

Sardinia

Similarly, Socrates 3.5 has a man named Lucifer as "bishop of Carala, a city of Sardinia"[22] and Theodoret 2.12 "Luciferus, bishop of the metropolis of the Isles of Sardinia." Sozomen also mentions "Lucifer, bishop of Cagliari in Sardinia."[23]

Antioch

Antioch exercised some sort of jurisdiction over Edessa. When heretics were causing problems at Edessa, the bishop of Antioch brought them to his city and "convicted them in their denial of their heresy." [24] In Theodoret 5.4, the bishop of Antioch ordained a man to the pastorate for Edessa, yet Edessa had its own representative at the (First) Council of Constantinople.[25]

Except that congregational bishops were more common than diocesan, there was no uniformity in structure for all geographic areas. The only general rule that can be drawn is enunciated by Sozomen 7.19:

> They faithfully and justly assumed, that those who accorded in the essentials of worship ought not to separate from one another on account of customs. For exactly similar traditions on every point are to be found in all the churches, even though they hold the same opinions. There are, for instance, many cities in Scythia, and yet

---

21. Socrates Scholasticus 5.24.
22. Socrates Scholasticus 3.5.
23. Sozomen 5.12.
24. Theodoret 4.10.
25. Theodoret 5.8.

they all have but one bishop;[26] whereas, in other nations a bishop serves as priest even over a village, as I have myself observed in Arabia, and in Cyprus, and among the Novatians and Montanists of Phrygia. Again, there are even now but seven deacons at Rome, answering precisely to the number ordained by the apostles, of whom Stephen was the first martyr; whereas, in other churches, the number of deacons is a matter of indifference. . . . Many other customs are still to be observed in cities and villages; and those who have been brought up in their observance would, from respect to the great men who instituted and perpetuated these customs, consider it wrong to abolish them.[27]

CONCLUSION

The various forms of church government above the congregation must have been rooted in something other than a divine rule or uniform tradition from the apostles. More likely is the secular government's desire for unity and stability. The relevant guidance here is from Tertullian:[28] the fact that postapostolic Christians agreed on certain things indicates that these things were handed down intact from apostolic times, for if all had departed from the original faith, they would have evolved differently and randomly and thus contradicted each other. Ecclesiastical polity during and after Constantine illustrates such randomness and differences.

The Roman emperor convoked a synod attended by four hundred churchmen in Ariminum (Rimini) in AD 359. In an argument about inter-episcopal councils and the creeds they espoused, one party denounced the position of the other on the grounds that it was contrary to "the ancient traditions of the Church, by which the churches had been governed by themselves."[29] Thus even in

26. Remember that Scythia was not absorbed into the Roman Empire until after the First Council of Nicaea.

27. Sozomen 7.19.

28. Tertullian, *Praescr.* 28.

29. Sozomen 4.17.

the mid-fourth century, bishops acknowledged that in early times local churches were autonomous rather than subject to metropolitans. They were probably not local chapels some distance from the main church of the bishop, or cathedral, collectively governed by a regional bishop. Without such chapels of convenience, "all who live in cities or in the country gather together to one place" as stated by Justin Martyr.[30] The New Testament "house churches" in the same city could not have had a single bishop apiece presided over by a bishop of the city, because it was considered forbidden or irregular for a city to have more than one bishop.[31] Canon 21 of the Council of Elvira prescribed punishment on city-dwellers who did not attend public worship for three Sundays, which bespeaks more than ordinary sloth and neglect, but there was no penalty for country-dwellers, who had a harder time to travel to the church building. This would imply that the conditions Justin mentioned still obtained in the early third century, and possibly into the fourth.

On the other hand, Robert M. Grant thought that leaders of city congregations exercised some sort of oversight in nearby areas even at the beginning of the second century.[32] Support for this view can be drawn from Ignatius in speaking of himself as "the bishop of Syria" (τὸν ἐπίσκοπον Συρίας), not just Antioch,[33] and of the church of the City of Rome as possessing "the presidency in the country of the land of the Romans" (προκάθηται ἐν τόπῳ χωρίου Ῥωμαίων).[34] Then again, he departed from his other letters by not mentioning a bishop or presbyter at Rome.[35] Two centuries later, Eusebius indicated τῶν κατὰ Γαλλίαν δὲ παροικιῶν, ἃς Εἰρηναῖος ἐπεσκόπει, which NPNF 2d translates as "the parishes in Gaul of which Irenaeus was bishop."[36] The Greek more precisely

---

30. Martyr, 1 Apol. 67.

31. Socrates 6.22; Sozomen 4.15; 5.3; Theodoret 2.14; Cyprian, Ep. 44.2, 46.

32. Grant, Augustus to Constantine, 154.

33. Ign. Rom. 2.2.

34. Ign. Rom. introduction.

35. Grant, Augustus to Constantine, 148.

36. Eusebius, Church History 5.23.2.

carries the meaning that he headed more than one of the churches in the province, perhaps all of them.[37] However, these expressions are dwarfed by the much greater number of statements that a bishop was over only one congregation, which would lead to the conclusion that Ignatius and Eusebius were speaking synoptically or laconically, to give readers the more approximate location of a place. Remember that there are two Antiochs in the New Testament. In addition, Eusebius may have used terminology that was current at the time he wrote, when many bishoprics were moving from congregational to diocesan.

37. Rev. Dr. David MacLachlan, email to author on 24 November 2020. He is Associate Professor for New Testament Studies, Atlantic School of Theology, Halifax, Nova Scotia.

CHAPTER 5

Electing and Deposing Clergy

THE AUTONOMY OF A LOCAL congregation is manifested in its right to choose and dismiss its own leaders. The following chapter reviews the substance and procedures of church government to outline the transition of the office of bishop from congregational and loss of this independence between New Testament times and the fifth century.

THE FIRST CENTURY

Acts 14:23 records that Paul and Barnabas ordained elders with prayer and fasting in every church of a missionary field, but does not comment on why particular individuals were selected for ordination, or the duties or powers granted to these new church officers. From Acts 15 it appears that elders filled some sort of important deliberative role with apostles.

In 1 Timothy 1:3, 4:6, and 11, and 2 Timothy 2:2 and 2:14, the apostle Paul is depicted as instructing his convert and younger colleague Timothy to perform tasks that in other places in the New Testament were those of an apostle. Such delegations of specific authorities witness the link between the apostles and later Christians.

The earliest reference seen as supporting the doctrine of apostolic succession is 2 Timothy 2:2, which relates that Paul conferred all or some of the apostolic capacities on a Christian of a younger generation, especially the teaching office: "And the things that thou hast heard of me among many witnesses, the same commit thou to faithful men, who shall be able to teach others also." Note the reference to a third generation, who were to carry on this teaching into another century. This does not specify bishops or elders of a local congregation, which were interchangeable designations in this time period, and relates to teaching and doctrine, not church government or discipline, or the validity of sacraments. A line of ordinations must begin with an apostle, but from 1 Timothy 4:14 and 2 Timothy 1:6 it is unclear whether Timothy was ordained by a college of presbyters or by the apostle Paul alone.

The next reference is in the Epistle to Titus. According to the King James Version, Paul purportedly commanded: "For this cause left I thee in Crete, that thou shouldest set in order the things that are wanting, and ordain elders in every city, as I had appointed thee" (Titus 1:5). The Douay-Rheims American Edition (1899) has "shouldest ordain priests in every city." The NRSV and NASB translate as "appoint elders." The root verb in the Greek is καθισημι. It has a wide range of translations in English New Testaments, but the only two uses in the context of causing someone to become a religious officeholder are the Old Testament high priest in Hebrews 5:1, 7:28, 8:3, and the selection and installation of the seven "deacons" in Act 6:3. In the latter case, the apostles in Acts 6:5 left the nomination of candidates to "the whole multitude," i.e., the Christian congregation. Titus was commanded to appoint presbyters, not necessarily bishops, and not necessarily without prior approval by the laypeople to be affected.

Because of the presence of apostles throughout the New Testament, its polity could not be a model for church order in the later periods in regard to one elder (bishop) placed above his fellow elders. Early post-Biblical Christian literature provides a more comparable model for later times, a model in which modern spiritual conditions are paralleled but with the added benefit of fresher memories of the apostles and their original institutions.

The Council of Acts 15 and the composition of 1 Clement took place in the time of the apostles, who had been directly commissioned by Christ and still received fresh visions from him. They possessed divine authority when issuing instructions. Their expertise was unique, and the postbiblical literature does not envision that apostolic authority or the office of apostles would continue.

The Didache 15.1 exhorts local Christian congregations themselves, not diocesan bishops or a pope, to select clergy: "Appoint, therefore, for yourselves, bishops and deacons worthy of the Lord, men meek, and not lovers of money, and truthful and proved; for they also render to you the service of prophets and teachers."

ELECTION OF CLERGY

Canon 4 of the First Council of Nicaea appears to abolish election by the laity. In practice, lay election continued with significant exceptions, and restrictions were placed on it. [1] This was not democracy as we understand it, for the bishop's term was for life, without opportunity for periodic elections with fixed terms and recalls by the voters.[2]

The Nicene period also witnesses the beginning of government intervention in election and deposition. An important feature was the birth of the notion that bishops assembled in intercongregational councils could elect a bishop.

> It is by all means proper that a bishop should be appointed by all the bishops in the province; but should this be difficult, either on account of urgent necessity or because of distance, three at least should meet together, and the suffrages of the absent [bishops] also being given and communicated in writing, then the ordination should

1. Norton, *Episcopal Elections*, 80, 243–44.

2. 1 Clem. 44; Cyprian, *Ep.* 67.5; Freeman, *New History*, 266; Norton, *Episcopal Elections*, 4.

take place. But in every province the ratification of what is done should be left to the Metropolitan.[3]

The Council of Nicaea presumes synods, church canons, and the office of metropolitan as well-established, just as Ignatius presumed monepiscopacy. It cites tradition and custom in support of many of its decrees, as if they possessed the same authority as scripture. Such tradition cannot have dated from the apostles, for it nowhere appears in the earlier literature, and varied from place to place.

At least for northern Africa and the West, all the attendees at Nicaea appear to have been metropolitan bishops, rather than leaders of single local congregations or even of small dioceses. We know the Christian world contained far more bishops than attended, which would indicate they came from only the top leadership, such as metropolitans or bishops chosen from regional groupings of far more bishops. Only one attendee each came from Gaul, Spain, and Proconsular Africa, while two presbyters represented Rome. In contrast, a synod of eighty-seven bishops assembled at Carthage under the presidency of Cyprian in 256. Fifteen to twenty years before Nicaea, but after the Diocletian Persecution, nineteen bishops and twenty-six presbyters attended the Council of Elvira in Spain.[4] About the same time, a synod at Rome was attended by three bishops of Gaul and fifteen from Italy, including the bishop of Rome.[5] Forty-three prelates attended a council in Gaul in AD 314 called by Constantine.[6] The *Epistle Catholic* 3 of Bishop Alexander of Alexandria narrates that there were nearly one hundred bishops in Egypt and Libya, but only twenty attended the First Council of Nicaea. Without citing an ancient authority, Gibbon estimated there were eighteen hundred catholic bishops in the Empire at the time of the Council,[7] while a little over three hundred attended it.

3 First Council of Nicaea, Canon 4.

4. See "Synod of Elvira."

5. Optatus of Milevis, *Contr. Don.* 1.23, written about AD 373.

6. See "Council of Arles of 314" and "Council of Arles."

7. Gibbon, *History of the Decline and Fall*, 2:279, 282.

According to J. Spencer Trimingham, "The fact that of the many bishops of the Province of Arabia five only attended the Council of Nicaea shows that there was then a distinction among its bishops."[8] It is no wonder the Nicaean Canons are so favorable to the powers of metropolitans, including veto over election of bishops, for many of the council fathers themselves were metropolitans. No one attendee is reported to have been directly elected by the laity.

The regional Council of Laodicea (AD 363–64), attended by thirty churchmen, reaffirmed the bare letter of the First Council of Nicaea: "Bishops are to be appointed to the ecclesiastical government by the judgment of the metropolitans and neighbouring bishops, after having been long proved both in the foundation of their faith and in the conversation of an honest life."[9] Its Canon 57 bears testimony that bishops had been congregational at one point, and is a classic statement of the growth of the new hierarchical arrangement:

> Bishops must not be appointed in villages or country districts, but visitors; and those who have been already appointed must do nothing without the consent of the bishop of the city. Presbyters, in like manner, must do nothing without the consent of the bishop.[10]

However, the *Synodical Letter of First Council of Constantinople* regards the provisions of Canon 4 as a "custom" among mortals, not an unchangeable requirement of God:

> Now as to the particular administration of individual churches, an ancient custom, as you know, has obtained, confirmed by the enactment of the holy fathers at Nicæa, that, in every province, the bishops of the province, and, with their consent, the neighbouring bishops with them, should perform ordinations as expediency may require. In conforming with these customs note that other

---

8. Trimingham, *Christianity among the Arabs*, 214.

9. Council of Laodicea, Canon 12.

10. Council of Laodicea, Canon 57.

churches have been administered by us and the priests of the most famous churches publicly appointed.[11]

The most common practice after Nicaea was for the people to choose a candidate, subject to the veto of the metropolitan or an ecumenical council through refusing to ordain.[12] In one case, according to Socrates Scholasticus, "Perigenes was ordained bishop of Patræ: but inasmuch as the inhabitants of that city refused to admit him, the bishop of Rome directed that he should be assigned to the metropolitan see of Corinth, which had become vacant by the decease of its former bishop."[13]

Sozomen 2.19 reports that, in support of a particular candidate, the emperor Constantine cited the candidate's acceptability by the people, which indicates the laity were a force to be taken into account. Sometimes a council of bishops, including an ecumenical council, deposed a bishop and nominated, elected, and ordained another person in his place, sometimes with nominal reference to laity.[14] Socrates 4.26 records that the bishop of one locality was elected by many bishops to be bishop of Constantinople. Athanasius was ordained without consulting the laity or all the bishops of the jurisdiction.[15] In some other instances, bishops were commissioned to elect in addition to their powers to ordain.[16]

The highwater mark of confining elections to other bishops occurred when John Chrysostom, bishop of Constantinople from AD 398 to 404, went to ordain a new bishop for Ephesus, but he found that

> the people were divided in their choice, some proposing one person, and some another, John perceiving that both parties were in a contentious mood, and that they did not wish to adopt his counsel, he resolved without much

11. From Theodoret 5.9.

12. Socrates Scholasticus 7.28; Sozomen 1.24; 8.2; Theodoret 1.8; Norton, *Episcopal Elections*, 39.

13. Socrates Scholasticus 7.36.

14. Theodoret 5.8; see also 1.6.

15. Sozomen 2.17.

16. Sozomen 4.25; 7.7.

ado to end their dispute by preferring to the bishopric a certain Heraclides, a deacon of his own, and a Cypriot by descent. And thus both parties desisting from their strife with each other had peace.[17]

Here, the laity's choice was deliberately overridden. A necessary decision, but out of step with the established protocol of the earlier church.

The Roman Emperors asserted certain rights over nominations and elections, but left the ordination ceremony to bishops.[18] At least once, an Emperor proposed two candidates for bishop, and "commanded the bishops to decide for one or other of them, or for whomsoever might appear worthy of the honor, and to ordain a president for the Church of Antioch."[19] During a vacancy in the bishopric of Constantinople, "the emperor commanded the priests to draw up a list of the names of those whom they thought worthy of the ordination, reserving to himself the right of choosing any one of those whose names were thus submitted to him."[20] The Emperor Constantius once complained because a man had been ordained without first consulting him. His Majesty, however, "returned to Antioch, without having either confirmed or dissolved his ordination."[21]

DEPOSING CLERGY

The opposite side of the coin from choosing a particular person to be bishop is the capacity to fire or depose him, whatever the wishes of the laity or other body that appointed him. Normally, the two powers go hand in hand. Congregations or sees are not autonomous if the duly chosen and ordained person set over them can be removed by outsiders. Yet, this is what we observe after

17. Socrates Scholasticus 6.11.
18. Sozomen 2.19.
19. Sozomen 2.19.
20. Sozomen 7.8.
21. Sozomen 3.7.

Constantine adopted Christianity. Unlike the first two centuries after the apostles, Christian churches no longer possessed self-determination or the right to choose their own leadership. To further the agendas of the secular government, only clergy who favored imperial policies would be appointed to the offices of bishop and metropolitan.

In the pre-Decian era, an election/ordination could never be rescinded, not even by the people who had elected him or the bishops who had ordained him: a bishop's term was for life.[22] Remember the whole purpose of 1 Clement was to deny that a congregation could remove their incumbent leaders and institute new ones. Prior to the introduction of monepiscopacy, the author(s) of 1 Clement attempted to persuade members of the church at Corinth to reinstate congregational leaders whom they had displaced in a revolt.

As enunciated by Cyprian, there was no bishop of bishops, nor could one bishop exact obedience from another, nor judge another.[23]

The testimony of 1 Clement and Cyprian in this regard is corroborated by the remarkable absence of evidence of bishops' attempting to depose other bishops from office during the Paschal Controversy of the late second century or similar serious pre-Constantinian inter-episcopal disputes wherein both sides accused the other of irregularities. They merely suspended communion with each other, without attempting to remove bishops they deemed unorthodox. Even during the schisms of Hippolytus and Novatian in the third century, the rival bishops did not purport to replace a duly consecrated officeholder but argued that their competitor had never been validly elected or ordained. In the schism involving Hippolytus, not even neighboring congregations intervened to heal the rift by removing the one who was not the rightful bishop or otherwise imposing a settlement. The implication is that they

22. 1 Clem. 44; Cyprian, *Ep.* 67.5; Freeman, *New History*, 266; Norton, *Episcopal Elections*, 4.

23. Cyprian's introductory remarks at the Seventh Council of Carthage, 1 September 258.

lacked the jurisdictional ability to do so. Even in other circumstances where they were most likely to do so, opposing bishops and congregations never purported to depose a bishop from his life appointment on the grounds of tyranny or corruption. With the debatable exception of Paul of Samosata, in no case was a bishop effectually removed by other Christians, and even this was by a pagan emperor after Paul had sided with an unsuccessful enemy of Rome, in an era when many Christians regarded the Roman Empire as an agency of Satan.

The first extant instance of outsiders refusing to recognize the legitimacy of a bishop dates from Cyprian, with bishops not allowed to return to their status after apostasy[24] and schism.[25] This was not unseating incumbent bishops but denying reinstatement after they had left the main body of the Catholic Church, or Christianity itself.

Writing of Novatian, Cyprian in *Epistle* 55.24 opined that a bishop lost episcopal status and capacity if he separated himself from the unity of bishops in the known world. According to Cyprian, schism put such a bishop outside the church, and he was no longer a Christian. However, such a factor was unnecessary to Cyprian's reasoning, what lawyers call *obiter dicta*, because Novatian had been ordained to the see of Rome after Cornelius had already been lawfully elected and ordained; another bishop was already in place for that congregation. Despite his opposition to Novatian, Cyprian did not indicate that there existed ecclesiastical mechanisms to stop him or intervene in his activities, nor did he advocate measures to prevent him from acting.

In the era between Cyprian and Constantine, the only instance of an attempt to depose a bishop by a council or other outside source was Paul of Samosata. However, the relevant councils could merely excommunicate Paul.[26] Excommunication is what Victor of Rome sought to do against the bishops of Proconsular Asia: if they approached him for communion in his own city, he

24. Cyprian, *Epp.* 65, 67.

25. Cyprian, *Ep.* 68.

26. Eusebius, *Church History* 7.29.1; 7.30.17; Theodoret 1.3.

would refuse to give it to them there; he would not go to Asia to remove them from their church buildings or end their government over their congregations. Excommunications were frequent in this era, without anyone being deposed or expelled. Another example is that of Demetrius's first synod against Origen: the excommunication did not annul Origen's ordination as presbyter. Demetrius did this later as an afterthought, at another council, which had no effect in Palestine where Origen conducted his ensuing presbyterial ministry. Granted, the synod attempted to depose Paul, but was ecclesiastically unsuccessful.

The laity still elected bishops with the disturbances earlier discountenanced by Origen, or at least exercised a veto over candidates unsatisfactory to them. The canon of the First Council of Nicaea that only bishops could elect other bishops was little observed in the time period of which Socrates Scholasticus wrote. He records the laity debating the merits of nominees for bishop (6.11), refusing to accept a proposed bishop and electing someone else (5.15), and expressing dissatisfaction with a nomination by an incumbent for his successor (5.21). The closest post-Nicene adherence to the canon is that people could elect their clergy, but only subject to confirmation by the bishop of Alexandria[27] or Constantinople.[28] The laity also exercised power to invest[29] or refuse to accept a new bishop.[30] This is contradicted by the instance of John Chrysostom inserting his own candidate when the laity could not agree among themselves, but this must be one of the customs—strong a custom as it was—that Sozomen 7.19 alluded to and confirms that the manner of proceeding was not uniform and therefore not descended from the apostles.

Bishops could not validly convey their office on their deathbed or by last will and testament,[31] something earlier discountenanced by Origen.

27. Sozomen 1.24.
28. Socrates Scholasticus 7.28.
29. Socrates Scholasticus 2.44.
30. Socrates Scholasticus 7.36.
31. Theodoret 5.23; Sozomen 7.14.

What was considered necessary to become a legitimate bishop are summarized in negative terms for rejecting an Arian claiming to be one: "No synod of orthodox bishops had chosen him; no vote of genuine clergy; no laity had demanded him; as the laws of the church enjoin."[32]

In post-Nicene times, councils of bishops, including ecumenical councils, deposed a host of bishops in total.[33] A Synod at Seleucia deposed eighteen bishops and a presbyter, some for no reason other than failing to attend the synod.[34]

One bishop was deposed and reinstated several times.[35] Five bishops were deposed three times, only to be restored when the times changed.[36] Even a pope of Rome was included in a deposition by a council of eastern bishops,[37] only to participate in a later synod of western bishops who restored him and those deposed with him, and in turn deposed eight bishops of the synod which had deposed them.[38] The whole of Sozomen's long chapters 4.24–25 are devoted to the names, sees, and offences of bishops and one deacon deposed by a council.

Almost invariably, the targets of councils of bishops were other bishops. An exception was when a council deposed a deacon for heresy.[39] This puzzles me, for the *Didascalia* and Hippolytus's *Apostolic Tradition* are abundantly clear that a deacon is his bishop's errand-boy, appointed by and answerable only to him, totally within his jurisdiction alone, exclusive even of his presbyters.[40] It is a serious transgression to give orders to the servant of someone

---

32. Theodoret 4.19.

33. Socrates Scholasticus 1.24, 36; 2.40; Sozomen 2.19, 33; 3.5–6, 11–12; 4.24–25; 8.6.

34. Socrates Scholasticus 2.40.

35. Socrates Scholasticus 4.12.

36. Theodoret 2.18.

37. Sozomen 3.11.

38. Sozomen 3.12.

39. Sozomen 4.24; Theodoret 2.24.

40. See chapter 6 of this book.

else, or to meddle in the relationship between them, and there is no power to dismiss from another's employment.

Socrates summarized the councils' atmosphere and manner of proceeding "this is a matter of common occurrence; the bishops are accustomed to do this in all cases, accusing and pronouncing impious those whom they depose, but not explaining their warrant for so doing."[41]

On their own initiative, some Roman emperors deposed or expelled bishops,[42] including the pope of Rome.[43] In at least one case, the emperor threatened to do so,[44] and declined a request to depose in another.[45] Constantine in one instance deposed a bishop and invited election of a replacement.[46] On the other side of the deposition process, the emperor Gratianus commanded the return of all deposed and exiled bishops in communion with Rome, and their church buildings restored.[47]

There was even a case of one bishop alone deposing another bishop: "Acacius of Cæsarea seized some small occasion, deposed Cyrillus, and drove him from Jerusalem."[48]

The church councils and synods mentioned in Socrates, Sozomen, and Theodoret appear not to be permanent, ongoing, strata of ecclesiastical governance, but convened for a specific purpose, usually an individual heresy or the (alleged) misbehavior of a particular person, mainly bishops. There is no record that such assemblies had permanent or fixed membership, but sometimes had overlapping membership with similar assemblies. Sometimes bishops on the losing side at one synod would not accept the decision of the majority, but assembled another synod of bishops more

41. Socrates Scholasticus 1.24.
42. Socrates Scholasticus 2.16; Theodret 2.12, 21, 25; 4.12.
43. Theodoret 4.11.
44. Theodoret 2.23.
45. Theodoret 1.19.
46. Socrates Scholasticus 1.9.
47. Theodoret 5.2.
48. Theodoret 2.22.

in accord with their opinion.[49] Nevertheless, they purported to accept and remove bishops who had been elected by their congregations and canonically ordained in keeping with the protocols of the earlier church, which these later bishops were violating.

49. E.g., Barnes, *Constantine and Eusebius*, 205.

CHAPTER 6

Who Became the Local Leaders under Diocesan Episcopacy?

THERE IS MODERN-DAY SPECULATION ON the mechanics of transition of the bishopric from congregational to diocesan in the period between Cyprian and the reign of Constantine. People who write on such matters assume that at the end of the process it was presbyters who became the local clergy in areas inconveniently distant from the bishop's residence or cathedral church. It may be that we are looking in the wrong place for the rank of church officers who became heads of parishes, and thus the innovation of a higher level of ecclesiastical government.

The instituting of local clergy other than the bishop may have been rooted in the diocesan diaconate, once the lowest rank in monepiscopacy but later provided the heads of congregations in a diocese. Justin Martyr records that it was the deacons who took Holy Communion from the community Eucharist to the absent, thus traveling more than presbyters on the congregation's behalf.[1] A few decades later, the only officer from Vienne in the *Letter of the Churches of Vienne and Lyons* is a deacon,[2] which indicates

1. Martyr, *1 Apol.* 67.
2. Eusebius, *Church History* 5.1.17; Telfer, *Office of a Bishop*, 96.

a deacon may have been the minister of this town, although this point cannot be stressed, given the scarcity of our information on the relationship between the two congregations. The authors of Epistle 67 in the Cyprianic collection wrote to a deacon as the presiding officer of a church in Spain as well as to its laity; however they also wrote to a presbyter as leader and the laity of two cities, and it is improbable but nevertheless possible that this presbyter was in charge of both because they were fifty kilometers apart. Be this as it may, the circumstances show that a deacon was equally a resident leader with a presbyter. After the Persecution of Diocletian but before the First Council of Nicaea, Canon 77 of the Council of Elvira speaks of a deacon serving a community without a bishop or presbyter, at least for baptism. The Canon foreshadows baptism by a resident minister, and confirmation only later by a bishop who makes a special trip. A few years later, Arles Canon 16 (15) acknowledges that deacons were already "conducting services in many places," but imposed the restriction that "this ought to happen as little as possible." Here is evidence that deacons were authorized, although grudgingly, to conduct liturgies distant from the cathedral city. Nor is the Canon clear whether the objection was against deacons conducting them at all, or that they did not restrict themselves to a single congregation but traveled around to more than one.

Three passages in Ignatius appear to reveal a higher regard for deacons than for presbyters, while consistently holding to the bishop as chief officer. He ranked deacons as trustees of the ministry and appointees of Christ higher than elders as apostles, in terms consistently a lower status than deacons:

> your bishop presides in the place of God, and your presbyters in the place of the assembly of the apostles, along with your deacons, who are most dear to me, and are entrusted with the ministry of Jesus Christ.[3]
>
> let all reverence the deacons as an appointment of Jesus Christ, and the bishop as Jesus Christ, who is the

---

3. Ign. *Magn.* 6.1.

Son of the Father, and the presbyters as the sanhedrim of
God, and assembly of the apostles.[4]

See that ye all follow the bishop, even as Jesus Christ
does the Father, and the presbytery as ye would the apostles; and reverence the deacons, as being the institution
of God.[5]

In commenting on an arrangement so contrary to what has
been generally assumed, Robert M. Grant refers to an inference by
a 1956 author who attributed Ignatius's arrangement to an earlier
church structure at Antioch consisting only of bishops and deacons, with the office of presbyters introduced later.[6] If anything,
the Bible indicates precisely the opposite, when it lists the requirement of both elders and deacons in 1 Timothy for Ephesus, but
only those for elders in Crete, as if deacons were unknown there,
but may reveal that the threefold ministry was not geographically
uniform in later New Testament times.

Be that as it may, Ignatius's extant words evince nothing that
there was any earlier arrangement. As his writings have come
down to us, Ignatius reveals that already around the turn of the
second century, monepiscopacy sometimes included a higher status for deacons than presbyters, which it was later natural to prefer
them as an order to represent bishops away from the cathedral city.

LeBreton and Zeiller speculate that local centers under the
control of presbyters or "priests" were established to accommo-
date Christians residing in distant parts of a bishop's territory who
would need to make a long journey to attend the cathedral church
in his home community. Because these centers had at first a teaching or catechetical, rather than a liturgical character, sometimes a
mere deacon would suffice. As a further development, a resident
local priest or presbyter later substituted for the bishop for pur-
poses of worship and administration at these centers, which were
afterwards called "parishes."[7]

4. Ign. *Trall.* 3.1.
5. Ign. *Smyrn.* 8.1.
6. Grant, *Augustus to Constantine*, 148.
7. LeBreton and Zeiller, *History of the Primitive Church*, 2:1112.

My difference with LeBreton and Zeiller is that the local deacons remained for a longer time period than they postulate, and also celebrated the sacraments at their bishops' behest. Remember that Ign. *Smyrn.* 8.1 does not tie the bishop's hands in the kinds of congregational officer or lay member to appoint to celebrate the Eucharist, much less limit him to presbyters.

Although subordinating deacons to presbyters in sacramental roles, Hippolytus's *Apostolic Tradition* and the *Didascalia* envision the deacons as more mobile and more involved with administration of the parish throughout its whole territory than the presbyters, and more likely to travel and remain in distant places at the bidding of the bishop. According to the *Apostolic Tradition*, deacons were to assemble in the presence of the bishop every day,[8] and be alert on his behalf.[9] The *Didascalia* outlines the deacon's non-liturgical duties, giving a picture of how he or she acts as a servant for the bishop, managed weekday affairs, and reported to him. The deacon received the laity's offerings and forwarded them to the bishop;[10] acted as a conduit for the laity's communications to him, with laity restricted to communicating with the bishop through deacons;[11] collected information about the parish and conveyed it to the bishop, such as who is in distress;[12] visited and provided for the sick and infirm;[13] knew all members of the congregation;[14] and taught.[15]

In the earliest eras of the church, deacons—but not presbyters—shared some powers with the bishop over the faithful. The Didache provides that local congregations appoint bishops and deacons, but seemingly not presbyters, as prophets.[16] In the early

---

8. Hippolytus, *Trad. ap.* 33.1 in Dix's numbering.

9. Hippolytus, *Trad. ap.* 30 in Dix's numbering.

10. *Didascalia* 9.

11. *Didascalia* 9.

12. *Didascalia* 9, 18.

13. *Didascalia* 16, 18.

14. *Didascalia* 16.

15. *Didascalia* 16.

16. Did. 15.1.

third century, these powers included inquiring when a complaint is brought against a Christian, and rebuking and judging backsliders.[17] In a more particular age than our own as regards church income, deacons were in charge of investigating the characters of people who offered to give to the church.[18] As for enrolled widows who dedicated themselves to church work and were supported by the congregation, *Didascalia* 15 stipulates that they are to first seek the permission of a bishop or a deacon before they eat or drink with anyone, fast with anyone, lay hands on anyone, pray over someone, or receive a gift from someone, thus indicating that deacons had more power than presbyters over members of the order of widows, a power shared only by bishops. Chapter 15 also instructs the aged women to obey bishops and deacons as God. Bishops had a duty to feed deacons, widows, and orphans from church funds,[19] with no similar provision for presbyters. Not being supported by the bounty of the bishop, presbyters could be more independent and less inclined to obey his directions than the deacons. Similarly, the "Notes" of Burton Scott Easton's translation of Hippolytus's *Apostolic Tradition* relate:

> The introduction of the local monarchical episcopate transformed the presbytery from the ruling body into a mere council of advice for the bishop, and so reduced radically the importance of its members. . . . Otherwise during the late second and third centuries their duties might be little more than honorary, and in most communities the presbyters probably devoted their weekdays to secular occupations; in contrast to the bishop and the deacons.[20]

The special relationship between bishops and deacons and their supremacy in church life to the exclusion of presbyters re-emerge in the Apostolic Constitutions.[21] These Constitutions had

17. *Didascalia* 10, 11.
18. *Didascalia* 18.
19. *Didascalia* 8–9.
20. Easton, *Apostolic Tradition of Hippolytus*, 77.
21. Apos. Con. 2:10, 30–32, 44.

a wider circulation and exercised more influence in the eastern church than the canons of councils.[22]

Linking bishop and deacon in a unity that did not include presbyters is demonstrated by a negative reference to the union, one that appears to demonstrate they were regarded as the paramount church officers in the public mind: the (gnostic) Apocalypse of Peter criticized people who called themselves "bishop" or "deacon."[23]

Along with the bishop, presbyters ordained new presbyters,[24] but the first eight verses of chapter 8 of the *Apostolic Tradition* constitute a treatise on why the bishop alone ordains deacons, and their sole dependence on him. The collegiality and higher sacramental and spiritual duties of presbyters as compared to the servile status of deacons would account for why the bishop would favor the latter as his local vicars in assemblies far from the cathedral city. Chapter 13 provides for the ordination of sub-deacons as assistants to the deacons, which would imply the deacons were more active and busier than presbyters, for there is no provision for "sub-presbyters."

Cyprian's third letter discloses the total subjection of deacons to the bishops' will, making them good choices as local vicars obedient to the bishop:

> deacons ought to remember that the Lord chose apostles, that is, bishops and overseers [episcopos et praepositos]; while apostles appointed for themselves deacons after the ascent of the Lord into heaven, as ministers of their episcopacy and of the Church. But if we may dare anything against God who makes bishops, deacons may also dare against us by whom they are made; and therefore it behoves the deacon of whom you write to repent of his audacity, and to acknowledge the honour of the priest [sacerdos], and to satisfy the bishop set over him with full humility.[25]

22. Norton, *Episcopal Elections*, 24.

23. Apoc. Pet. 79.

24. Hippolytus, *Trad. ap.* 7.1—8.8.

25. Cyprian, *Ep.* 64.3.

There may have been both deacons and presbyters in paramount local leadership roles, with the latter becoming more common through the years. Canon 1 of the Council of Antioch in AD 341 mentions "any one of those who preside in the Church, whether he be bishop, presbyter, or deacon." Like monepiscopacy, the previous revolution in ecclesiastical polity, diocesan episcopacy may well have happened at different times in different places, both before and after the First Council of Nicaea. Although well established, it was not yet universal in the fifth century.[26]

26. Sozomen 7.19.

Chapter 7

Observations

SURPRISINGLY, THERE ARE NO EXTANT records of opposition to either of these revolutions, nobody arguing that the developments were wrongful because they violated any divine or apostolic plan for church government. There were objections to particular candidates, but not to the congregational, presbyterial, or episcopal arrangement itself.

Christian people's acceptance of monopiscopacy and diocesan-hierarchical polity was not exacted by force or lay misgivings that it was improper and unchristian to voice dissent from initiatives from the leadership. Early Christians did not automatically follow their leaders even when they suspected them to be in error about church polity. The laity were not passive or apathetic on other issues, but could strongly and physically react to developments they did not like. This is illustrated by their active resistance and physical force in other areas of church life.

When the repenting apostates applied for reinstatement in the church after the Decian Persecution, the clergy required signs of sorrow and a period of waiting. The reaction of the lapsed was to threaten the clergy with bodily harm to coerce them.[1] A couple

---

1. Cyprian, *Laps.* 22.

of years later, in the Cornelius-Novatian schism, the clergy of the majority church were attacked by various groups and individuals, who assailed them with threats,[2] reproaches,[3] reviling,[4] and other abusive speech,[5] and even terrors[6] and armed violence.[7]

Neither bishops, secular rulers, nor the common people showed much respect for due order, obedience to constituted authority, or peaceful or diplomatic airing of differences. Socrates Scholasticus often records the laity tumultuously rejecting a candidate for bishop,[8] or disturbing the rule of an incumbent. Often the laity obtained their own way by rowdy behavior, and both secular and church authorities refrained from implementing a particular policy for fear of agitating the masses. The most concise examples are in Sozomen 3.6 and 3.7: "The indignation of the people was aroused, and they burnt the church which bore the name of Dionysius, one of their former bishops."[9] Sozomen 3.7 relates of a disputed episcopal election at Constantinople: "This excited frequent seditions in the city which assumed all the appearance of a war, for the fell upon one another, and many perished. The city was filled with tumult." More comprehensively, Charles Freeman, in commenting in episcopal elections in the fourth and fifth centuries, notes: "Almost every election of which we have records was a violent one."[10] The same was true of their deposition, with both accompanied by "public disorder and bloodshed . . . rioting and violence"[11] with clubs and swords.[12] Novatianists burst with clamor into solemn assemblies of the other party, who for their

2. Cyprian, *Ep.* 59.2, 17, 19, 21.

3. Cyprian, *Ep.* 59.2, 8.

4. Cyprian, *Ep.* 59.4.

5. Cyprian, *Ep.* 59.8, 19, 21.

6. Cyprian, *Ep.* 59.2, 17.

7. Cyprian, *Ep.* 59.2, 19.

8. Socrates Scholasticus 2.20; 4.29; 5.5.

9. Sozomen 3.6.

10. Freeman, *New History*, 266.

11. Norton, *Episcopal Elections*, 56.

12. Cyprian, *Ep.* 59.2.

own part refused to receive testimonies or written evidence or make the slightest attempt to look into their allegations.[13]

Sozomen also relates the behavior and its result concerning Hermogenes, a general, in his attempt to carry out the emperor Constantius's wish to undo an election. When Hermogenes tried to use force to remove the bishop from the church building, the result was that

> the people, instead of yielding, met him with open resistance, and while the soldiers, in order to carry out the orders they had received, attempted still greater violence, the insurgents entered the house of Hermogenes, set fire to it, killed him, and attaching a cord to his body, dragged it through the city.[14]

During the period material to the present book and for some centuries afterward, "The choice, appointment or forced installation (or deposition) of a bishop was one of the most common causes of public disorder and bloodshed in the cities of the late Empire."[15] Yet there was no similar objection to changing the organizational structure of the universal church, along the lines of bishops over several congregations and metropolitans over several bishops. In fact, the system of metropolitans was not finalized in the western Empire until decades, even a century in some places, later than its establishment in the east.[16]

For their own part, bishops of Socrates's era abused the institution of synod or council by refusal to hear both sides, deposing a bishop without a hearing, refusing to attend episcopal councils, attending only when they already knew their view would be adopted, or refusing to act because of private piques against the other bishops. In too many cases, bishops who were in the minority on a vote at one council gathered together colleagues more to their liking and held a synod with the opposite result. If this failed, some

---

13. Cyprian, *Ep.* 44.1.

14. Sozomen 3.7.

15. Norton, *Episcopal Elections*, 56.

16. Norton, *Episcopal Elections*, 244.

appealed to the secular authorities. Sometimes they adjourned a council before its stated business was completed, and against the express wish of the emperor. For their parts, emperors sometimes convoked or dissolved episcopal councils at their own pleasure. Some tried to appoint or depose a bishop on no more than their own secular authority, but met with riotous opposition from the people. Thus, the laity still elected bishops with the disturbances discountenanced by Origen in the third century, or at least exercised a veto over candidates unsatisfactory to them. Particular personalities and policies unrelated to church polity suffered contention and strong opposition, but not the structural framework itself.

Indeed, the author of *The Apostolic Tradition* described a framework for dissent and counteracting decisions of the leadership "in order that those who have been rightly instructed may hold fast to that tradition which has continued until now."[17] He assured his readers that "The Holy Ghost bestows the fulness of grace on those who believe rightly that they may know how those who are at the head of the Church should teach the tradition and maintain it in all things."[18] As the second quotation indicates, the laity were to be educated in the tradition so that they could evaluate the correctness of their clergy's teaching, presumably to take measures against those who deviated from it. Apparently, the people did not regard inter-congregational governance to be part of this tradition.

The exception to silence and acceptance of change in inter-congregational organization was when Stephen of Rome asserted in the AD 250s that as the only successor of the apostle Peter he had jurisdiction over the universal church, with the authority to intervene in local bishoprics. And thus the matter largely stands in our own day for the heirs of Constantinian episcopacy. Nor was there any constitutional document like *The Form of Presbyterian Church Government* in the *Westminster Standards* detailing officers and levels of government, their powers and responsibilities,

17. Hippolytus, *Trad. ap.* 1.3.
18. Hippolytus, *Trad. ap.* 1.5.

and their mutual relations. The ancients from the beginning of the church until at least the fifth century did not hold that there was only one divinely-approved pattern of church polity. It all depended on what the laity would acquiesce in.

Sketches of Early Sources Cited

Alexander of Alexandria. Metropolitan bishop of Alexandria in Egypt. Protagonist against Arianism before and at the First Council of Nicaea. Died AD 328.

Anatolius. Bishop of Laodicea-in-Syria, and of Alexandria. Died in AD 283.

Apostolic Constitutions. Anonymous collection on Christian conduct, church administration, and liturgy, drawing from *Didache*, *Didascalia*, and other sources. Compiled in late fourth century, probably in Syria.

Archelaus, bishop of Carrhae in Mesopotamia. Engaged in debates with Manes around AD 278, the extant record of which is probably fourth century.

Clement of Alexandria, Egypt. Foremost Christian thinker of his day. Principal or dean of the world's leading institute of higher learning in the AD 190s.

Constantine the Great, Roman emperor, AD 306–37. Embraced Christianity in AD 313 but was not baptized until his deathbed. Began as emperor of the West and became sole emperor in 324. First openly Christian emperor and generous benefactor of the church. Participated in church councils including I Nicaea and administration of the church. Attempted to keep Christianity united. In contrast to the previous, persecuting, emperors, he promoted the Catholic Church financially, in diplomacy, and organizationally.

Constantius II, emperor of the eastern Roman Empire AD 337 to 361, emperor of whole Empire from AD 350. Actively intervened in church matters, including many synods to promote Christian unity.

Cornelius, bishop of Rome, AD 251–53, martyr. Dealt with if and how to reconcile to the church Christians who had lapsed during the Decian Persecution, in contrast to Novatian and his followers who denied reconciliation was possible and generally favored a stricter Christian lifestyle.

Cyprian. Bishop of Carthage, Tunisia, ca. AD 248–58. Ordained bishop while still a neophyte, which caused friction with local elders/presbyters. Leading churchman of African Mediterranean shore from Libya to Morocco. Martyr.

Decius (adjective Decian), Roman emperor from AD 249 to 251, which period saw the most thoroughgoing persecution of Christianity to that date. Caused many Christians to apostatize by sacrificing to Roman deities on government orders.

Didache, or *Teaching of the Twelve Apostles*. Anonymous church manual written in Egypt or Syria in the first century or early second century AD, and may predate the Gospel of Matthew.

Didascalia Apostolorum. Church manual and code of church law compiled in the first three decades of the third century, probably in Syria, perhaps in Palestine.

Diocletian, Roman emperor from AD 284 to 305. Began the most extensive and efficient persecution of Christians.

Diodorus, presbyter in a town also named Diodorus. Associate of Archelaus, facilitating an AD 278 debate with Manes.

Eusebius, bishop of Caesarea in Palestine. One of Constantine's advisors on church matters. First major historian of Christianity. His long quotations of early sources preserve valuable early Christian documents not available elsewhere. Died ca. AD 339.

Firmilian, Bishop of Caesarea in Cappadocia. Letter to Cyprian, or Epistle 75 in the Cyprianic collection.

First Council of Constantinople, AD 381. Largely a synod of eastern bishops called by the Roman emperor. Reaffirmed the theology of I Nicaea.

First Council of Nicaea, AD 325. First ecumenical council, i.e., drawing representatives from all parts of the known world. Convened by the Emperor Constantine.

First Epistle of Clement Between AD 70 and 97. Letter from congregation at Rome to that at Corinth to reverse the replacement of elders and deacons in the apostolic tradition by ones more to some Corinthians' liking. Widely regarded as scripture in the early Christian centuries.

Gnostic Apocalypse of Peter. Gnostic. Late second century or early third century AD. Also called *Coptic Gnostic Apocalypse of Peter*. Not the same as the (Ethiopic) *Revelation of Peter*.

Hippolytus. Studied under Irenaeus. Presbyter in central Italy in early third century. Rival bishop of Rome, ca. AD 217–35.

Ignatius. Bishop of Antioch. Just before AD 107 he wrote letters to the church at Rome; to bishop Polycarp of Smyrna, and to five churches in the Aegean basin: Ephesus, Magnesia, Philadelphia, Smyrna, and Tralles. Martyr. First writer to propound monepiscopacy.

Irenaeus. Bishop of Lyons (France) in last quarter of the second century. Grew up a Christian in Smyrna (western Turkey), where he studied under Polycarp, who in turn had known the Apostle John.

Jerome, about AD 347 to 419/20. Scholar, monk, prodigious writer on Christian topics. Attended First Council of Constantinople.

Justin Martyr. Philosopher and teacher in a Christian school. Widely traveled. Flourished at Rome in the mid-second century AD.

Letter of the Churches at Vienne and Lyons to the Churches of Asia and Phrygia. Southern France. Shortly after AD 177.

Novatian. Leading presbyter of the city of Rome, and after AD 250 rival bishop of the city. Led the church party that advocated rigorism in penance and denied repentant apostates readmission to the church. His denomination persisted to the end of the period discussed in the present book.

Origen, AD 185–254/255. Foremost Christian theologian and teacher of the third century. The most prolific Christian writer prior to Martin Luther. Presbyter after AD 230. From AD 202 to 230 or 233 he was the dean/principal of the world's foremost institution of higher learning, as successor of Clement of Alexandria. In AD 231 or 233 Origen established his own at Caesarea in Palestine. Traveled much in the eastern Roman Empire as a theological consultant to local churches.

Polycarp. A disciple of the Apostle John and may have been the "angel of Smyrna" mentioned in Revelation 2:8. Western Turkey. First third of the second century.

Shepherd of Hermas. First half of second century. City of Rome. Collection of visions and teachings on the Christian life.

Socrates Scholasticus, also known as Socrates of Constantinople, where he resided his entire life. Lawyer who held no office in the church. His book covers the church from AD 305 to 439.

Sozomen, Salaminius Hermias. Church historian. Resided at Constantinople after AD 425. A layman critical of bishops. The extant text of his book describes church history from the second century to AD 440 or 443. Although three-quarters of the book depends on Socrates, it is a new work in which he added material from other sources and went back to the sources from which the earlier writer drew.

Stephen, bishop of Rome, AD 254–57. Tried to assert the supremacy of the bishop of Rome over all Christendom on the issue of whether converts to the Catholic Church from other denominations must be baptized again.

Tertullian. A lawyer in Rome who upon conversion to Christianity gave up secular law and became a presbyter in Tunisia. Later joined the Montanists, a rigorous denomination that condemned the mainline church for what it saw as slackness in religious observance and lack of enthusiasm. The most prolific ante-Nicene Christian author writing in Latin. Founder of Latin Christian literature. Wrote between AD 197 and 220.

Theodoret, bishop of Cyrrhus from AD 423. Scholar and active churchman also involved in secular matters. Well-educated in ecclesiastical history. His book ends at AD 429, although it was completed around AD 449, and contains material from sources other than Socrates and Sozomen.

Victor, bishop of Rome, AD 189–99. Tried to unify Christian practice as to the date of ending the Lenten fast and celebrating Easter.

Appendix

Finding Epistles by Number in Collection of Cyprian

THERE ARE TWO METHODS OF numbering for the collection of letters to and from Cyprian. One is that in Wilhelm August Hartel *S. Thasci Caecili Cypriani* : Opera omnia / *recensvit et commentario critico* (Vindobonae : apvd C. Geroldi filivm, 1868–71). Series: Corpus scriptorum ecclesiasticorum Latinorum (abbreviated "CSEL"), vol. 3. It is usually cited as CSEL. This numbering is obligatory for academic scholarship, but is sometimes found in literature for a more general readership. The other is that in *The Ante-Nicene Fathers: Translations of The Writings of the Fathers down to A.D. 325*. Edited by Alexander Roberts and James Donaldson. American reprint ed. by A. Cleveland Coxe (1885–96; continuously reprinted), abbreviated "ANF." Its numbering is common in works not meant for scholars, and is usual for writers who have not benefited from education in early Christian studies, or who seek a mass audience without such training, or have trouble reading CSEL on the internet, or cannot read Latin fluently.

Two systems of numbering understandably create confusion, especially when the author cites CSEL and the reader cannot read Latin, or wishes to consult the ANF for any reason. Citations to the

Appendix

ANF are less of a problem, because the first footnote to each letter in ANF indicates the CSEL number. To assist readers to find the number of the letter in ANF when the book they are reading cites only the CSEL, the following table is provided:

CSEL	ANF		CSL	ANF
1	65		25	19
2	60		26	17
3	64		27	22
4	61		28	24
5	4		29	23
6	80		30	30 (same)
7	35		31	25
8	2		32	31
9	3		33	26
10	8		34	27
11	7		35	28
12	36		36	29
13	6		37	15
14	5		38	32
15	10		39	33
16	9		40	34
17	11		41	37
18	12		42	38
19	13		43	39
20	14		44	40
21	20		45	41
22	21		46	43
23	16		47	42
24	18		48	44

Finding Epistles by Numberin Collection of Cyprian

CSEL	ANF
49	45
50	47
51	46
52	48
53	49
54	50
55	51
56	52
57	53
58	55
59	54
60	56
61	57
62	59
63	62
64	58
65	63
66	68
67	67 (same)
68	66
69	75
70	69
71	70
72	71
73	72
74	73
75	74
76	76 (same)
77	77 (same)
78	78 (same)
79	79 (same)
80	81
81	82

Bibliography

Alexander of Alexandria. *Epistle Catholic.* In ANF 6:296–99.

Anatolius of Laodicea. *Paschal Canon.* In ANF 6:146–51.

Apolinaris of Hierapolis. *Letter to Abircius Marcellus.* In In NPNF 2d 1:230–33.

Apostolic Constitutions, or *Constitutions of the Holy Apostles.* In ANF 7:385–505.

Archelaus. *Acts of the Disputation with the Heresiarch Manes.* In ANF 6:179–235.

Barnes, Timothy D. *Constantine and Eusebius.* Cambridge, MA: Harvard University Press, 1981.

Bigg, Charles. *The Christian Platonists of Alexandria: The 1886 Bampton Lectures.* Oxford: Clarendon, 1968.

Brennan, Juicio. "An Intriguing History: Election of Bishops in the Catholic Church." https://juiciobrennan.com/files/bishopselection/bishopSelectionFlier.pdf.

Bruce, Frederick Fyvie. *The Spreading Flame: The Rise and Progress of Christianity from Its First Beginnings to the Conversion of the English.* Greenwood, SC: Attic Press, 1978.

Bullard, Roger A., trans. *Gnostic Apocalypse of Peter.* In *The Nag Hammadi Library in English*, by James M. Robinson, 340–45. San Francisco: Harper & Row, 1981.

Churches at Vienne and Lyons. *Letter to the Churches of Asia and Phrygia.* In ANF 8:778–84.

Clement I, Pope. *First Epistle of Clement.* In ANF 1:[5]–21; ANF 10:[229]–48.

Clement of Alexandria. *Stromata.* In ANF 2:299–567.

Connolly, R. Hugh. *Didascalia Apostolorum: The Syriac Version Translated and Accompanied by the Verona Latin Fragments.* Oxford: Clarendon, 1929.

Council of Ancyra. *Canons.* In NPNF 2d 14:63–75.

"Council of Arles." https://www.britannica.com/event/Council-of-Arles.

"Council of Arles of 314." https://orthodoxwiki.org/Council_of_Arles_of_314.

Council of Laodicea. *Canons.* In NPNF 2d 14:[125]–34.

Council of Neocaesarea in Pontus. *Canons.* In NPNF 2d 14:79–86.

Cowper, B. Harris. *Syriac Miscellanies: Or Extracts Relating to the First and Second General Councils.* London: Williams & Norgate, 1861. http://www.tertullian.org/fathers/syriac_misc.htm#Theodorus.

Cyprian. *Epistulae,* or *Letters.* In ANF 5:267–409.

———. "[Introductory Remarks at] the Seventh Council of Carthage, 1 Sept 258." In ANF 5:575.

———. *On the Lapsed.* ANF 5:437–47.

Didache, or *Teaching of the Twelve Apostles.* In ANF 7:377–82.

Dionysius of Alexandria. *Letter to Sextus II of Rome.* In NPNF 2d 1:294–95.

Easton, Burton Scott. *The Apostolic Tradition of Hippolytus.* New York: Macmillan, 1934.

Eusebius. *Church History.* Translated by Arthur Cushman McGiffert. 14 vols. 1890. Reprint, Grand Rapids, MI: Eerdmans, 1997. In NPNF 2d 1:[1]–387.

———. *Life of Constantine.* In NPNF 2d 1:[481]–559.

———. *Panegyric to Constantine,* or *Oration of Eusebius Pamphilus in Praise of the Emperor Constantine.* In NPNF 2d 1:[581]–610.

Evans Grubbs, Judith. "'Pagan' and 'Christian' Marriage." *Journal of Early Christian Studies* 2 (1994) 361–412.

Ferguson, Everett, ed. *Encyclopedia of Early Christianity.* New York: Garland, 1990.

Firmilian. *Letter to Cyprian.* In ANF 5:390–97; Hartel 3:810–27.

Fiedler, Maureen. "Return to Early Church Practice—Elect Our Bishops." *National Catholic Reporter,* September 15, 2016. https://www.ncronline.org/blogs/ncr-today/return-early-church-practice-elect-our-bishops.

First Council of Constantinople. *Canons.* In NPNF 14:[172]–86.

———. *Synodical Letter.* In NPNF 2d 14:[188]–90.

First Council of Nicaea. *Canons.* In NPNF 2d 14:8–42.

Freeman, Charles. *A New History of Early Christianity.* New Haven: Yale University Press, 2011.

Frend, W. H. C. *The Donatist Church: A Movement of Protest in Roman North Africa.* Oxford: Clarendon, 1952.

———. *The Early Church.* Minneapolis: Fortress, 1982.

———. *The Rise of Christianity.* Philadelphia: Fortress, 1984.

Gibbon, Edward. *History of the Decline and Fall of the Roman Empire.* New York: Knopf, 1994.

Grant, Robert M. *After the New Testament.* Philadelphia: Fortress, 1967.

———. *Augustus to Constantine: the Rise and Triumph of Christianity in the Roman World.* Louisville, KY: Westminster John Knox, 2004.

Hartel, Wilhelm August. *S. Thasci Caecili Cypriani* : Opera omnia / *recensvit et commentario critico.* Corpus scriptorum ecclesiasticorum Latinorum. Vindobonae : apvd C. Geroldi filivm, 1868–71. 3 vols.

Hefele, Charles Joseph. *A History of the Christian Councils.* Translated by William R. Clark. 2nd ed. New York: AMS Press, 1972.

Hippolytus. *Apostolic Tradition.* http://www.bombaxo.com/hippolytus.html.

Bibliography

————. *The Treatise on the Apostolic Tradition.* Translated by Gregory Dix, reissued by Henry Chadwick. London: SPCK, 1968.

Huizing, Peter, and Knut Walf, eds. *Electing Our Own Bishops.* Edited in English by Marcus Lefébure. New York: Seabury, 1980.

Ignatius of Antioch. *Letter to the Magnesians.* In ANF 1:59–65.

————. *Letter to the Romans.* In ANF 1:73–78.

————. *Letter to the Smyrnaeans.* In ANF 1:86–92.

————. *Letter to the Trallians.* In ANF 1:66–72.

James, Montague Rhodes. *The Apocryphal New Testament.* 1953. Reprint, Oxford: Clarendon, 1963.

Jerome, Saint. *De Viris Illustribus [On Illustrious Men].* Translated by Thomas P. Halton. Washington, DC: Catholic University of America Press, 1999.

————. *Letter 146.* http://www.newadvent.org/fathers/3001146.htm.

————. *Letter 3.* https://www.newadvent.org/fathers/3001033.htm.

Kilmartin, Edward J. "Episcopal Election: The Right of the Laity." In *Electing Our Own Bishops,* edited by Peter Huizing and Knut Walf, 39–43. Edited in English by Marcus Lefébure. New York: Seabury, 1980.

Kostash, Myrna. "Once There Were Deaconesses." *Myrna Kostash* (blog), June 28, 2018. https://www.myrnakostash.com/once-there-were-deaconesses/.

Kretschmar, Georg. "The Councils of the Ancient Church." In *The Councils of the Church,* edited by Hans Jochen Margull, translated by Walter F. Bense, 14–81. Philadelphia: Fortress, 1966.

Lake, Kirsopp. *The Apostolic Fathers, with an English Translation.* 2 vols. Cambridge, MA: Harvard University Press, 1955.

Lane Fox, Robin. *Pagans and Christians.* New York: Knopf, 1987.

LeBreton, Jules, and Jacques Zeiller. *The History of the Primitive Church.* 2 vols. New York: Macmillan, 1949.

Martyr, Justin. *1 Apology.* In ANF 1:163–87.

Moore, Peter. "Reflections upon Reflections." In *Bishops, But What Kind? Reflections upon Episcopacy,* edited by Peter Moore, 162–76. London: SPCK, 1982.

Norton, Peter. *Episcopal Elections 250–600: Hierarchy and Popular Will in Late Antiquity.* New York: Oxford University Press, 2007.

O'Callaghan, Joseph F. *Electing Our Bishops: How the Catholic Church Should Choose Its Leaders.* Lanham, MD: Rowman & Littlefield, 2007.

Optatus of Milevis. *Against the Donatists.* http://www.tertullian.org/fathers/index.htm#Against_the_Donatists.

Origen. *Commentary on Ephesians.* In *The Commentaries of Origen and Jerome on St. Paul's Epistle to the Ephesians,* translated by Ronald E. Heine, 75–272. Oxford Early Christian Studies. Oxford: Oxford University Press, 2002.

————. *Dialogue with Heraclides.* In *Treatise on the Passover and Dialogue of Origen with Heraclides and his Fellow Bishops on the Father, the Son, and the Soul,* translated by Robert J. Daly, 57–78. New York: Paulist, 1992.

————. *Homélies sur les Nombres.* Edited by Louis Doutreleau. Paris: Cerf, 1996.

Bibliography

————. *Homélies sur les Nombres*. Translated by André Méhat. Paris: Cerf, 1951.

————. *Homilies on Isaiah*. In *Isaïe: Origène, Homélies traduites par Jacques Millet, Sermons d' Augustin, d'Eusèbe le Gallican, de saint Bernard, de Rupert de Deutz traduits par Jacqueline Legée et les Carmélites de Mazille*, 21–87. N.p.: Desclée de Brower, 1983.

————. *Homilies on Isaiah*. In *St. Jerome: Commentary on Isaiah*, translated by Thomas P. Scheck, 881–928. New York: Newman, 2015.

————. *Homilies on Leviticus*. Translated by Gary Wayne Barkley. Washington, DC: Catholic University of America Press, 1990.

————. *Homilies on Psalm 37*. In *Homélies sur les Psaumes 36 à 38*, translated by Henri Crouzel and Luc Brésard, 257–327. Paris: Cerf, 1995.

————. *Homilies on the Psalms: Codex Monacensis Graecus 314*. Translated and annotated by Joseph W. Trigg. Washington, DC: Catholic University of America Press, 2020.

Oulton, John Ernest Leonard, and Henry Chadwick. *Alexandrian Christianity: Selected Translations*. Philadelphia: Westminster Press, 1954.

Pastor of Hermas. In ANF 2:9–55.

Peter of Alexandria. *Letter to the Church at Alexandria*. In ANF 6:280.

Phileas of Thmuis. *The Epistle of the Same Phileas of Thmuis to Meletius, Bishop of Lycopolis*. In ANF 6:163–64.

Quasten, Johannes. *Patrology*. Westminster, MD: Christian Classics, 1950 reprinted 1986.

Roberts, Alexander, and James Donaldson. *The Ante-Nicene Fathers: Translations of the Writings of the Fathers Down to A.D. 325*. 10 vols. Buffalo, NY: Christian Literature, 1885–96.

Schaff, Philip, and Henry Wace. *Nicene and Post-Nicene Fathers, Second Series*. 14 vols. New York: Christian Literature, 1900.

Socrates Scholasticus. *Ecclesiastical History*. Revised and edited by Kevin Knight. https://www.newadvent.org/fathers/2601.htm.

Southern, Pat. *The Roman Empire from Severus to Constantine*. New York: Routledge, 2001.

Sozomen, Salaminius Hermias. *Ecclesiastical History*. Revised and edited by Kevin Knight. https://www.newadvent.org/fathers/2602.htm.

Stockmeier, Peter. "The Election of Bishops by Clergy and People in the Early Church." In *Electing Our Own Bishops*, edited by Peter Huizing and Knut Walf, 3–9. New York: Seabury, 1980.

Synod of Elvira. *Canons*. In *Morality and Ethics in Early Christianity*, by Jan L. Womer, 75–82. Philadelphia: Fortress, 1987.

"Synod of Elvira." https://en.wikipedia.org/wiki/Synod_of_Elvira.

Telfer, William. *Office of a Bishop*. London: Darton, Longman & Todd, 1962.

Tertullian. *De praescriptione haereticorum* [*The Prescription against Heretics*]. In ANF 3:243–65.

————. *On Fasting*. In ANF 4:102–14.

Bibliography

Theodoret of Cyrrhus. *Ecclesiastical History.* Revised and edited by Kevin Knight. https://www.newadvent.org/fathers/2702.htm.

Three Books to Abercius Marcellus, or *Against the Cataphrygians.* In ANF 7:335–37.

Trimingham, John Spencer. *Christianity among the Arabs in Pre-Islamic Times.* New York: Longmans, 1979.

Ware, Kallistos. "Patterns of Episcopacy in the Early Church and Today: An Orthodox View." In *Bishops But What Kind? Reflections upon Episcopacy,* edited by Peter Moore, 1–24. London: SPCK, 1982.

Westminster Assembly. "The Form of Presbyterian Church Government according to the Westminster Standards." https://www.apuritansmind.com/westminster-standards/form-of-presbyterian-church-government/.